scrap crochet™

General Information

Many of the products used in this pattern book can be purchased from local craft, fabric and variety stores, or from the Annie's Attic Needlecraft Catalog (see Customer Service information on page 48).

Contents

2 Quilt Rug

4 Sunflower Towel Topper & Dishcloth

6 Scrap Afghan

9 Ribbon Pillow

10 Carry-All Bag

11 Dishbottle Apron

12 Hot Pads

14 Daffodil Tea Cozy & Coasters

17 Trio of Trivets

21 Glass Cozies

22 Table Runner

24 Flowerberry

25 Tape Measure Covers

27 Blue Wrap

29 Glove Trims

30 Easy Anywhere Bag

32 Flame Necklace

34 Turtle

36 Bunny Booties

38 Scrap Jacket

42 Flower Bib & Booties

44 Teddy Bear Party Pinafore

46 Stitch Guide

47 Metric Conversion Charts

Quilt Rug

DESIGN BY **SHIRLEY BROWN**

SKILL LEVEL

INTERMEDIATE

FINISHED SIZE

30½ x 41 inches

MATERIALS

- Bernat Berella "4" medium (worsted) weight yarn (3½ oz/ 195 yds/100g per ball):
  9 balls #08994 black
  4 balls each #08886 light tapestry gold, #01222 fern, #01133 cobalt, #01310 lavender and #08929 geranium
- Size J/10/6mm crochet hook or size needed to obtain gauge
- Tapestry needle

GAUGE

5 sc = 2 inches; 5 sc rows = 2 inches

PATTERN NOTES

Hold 3 strands of same color together unless otherwise stated.

Always change color in last stitch.

Each square on chart equals one single crochet stitch.

Weave in ends as work progresses.

Join rounds with slip stitch unless otherwise stated.

INSTRUCTIONS

SQUARE
MAKE 4.

Row 1: **With 3 strands black held tog** (see *Pattern Notes*), ch 31, sc in 2nd ch from hook, sc in each rem ch across, **change color** (see *Stitch Guide and Pattern Notes*) to light tapestry gold in last sc, turn. *(30 sc)*

Rows 2–30: Ch 1, sc in each st across, changing colors according to chart, turn. At end of last row, fasten off.

CORNER
MAKE 4.

Row 1: With 3 strands of black held tog, ch 16, sc in 2nd ch from hook, sc in each rem ch across, turn. *(15 sc)*

Row 2: Ch 1, sc in each sc across to last 3 sc, **sc dec** (see *Stitch Guide*) in next 2 sts, sc in last st, turn. *(14 sc)*

Row 3: Ch 1, sc in each sc across, turn.

Rows 4–23: [Rep rows 2 and 3 alternately] 10 times. (*3 sc at end of last row*)

Row 24: Ch 1, sc in each sc across, turn.

Row 25: Rep row 24.

Row 26: Ch 1, sc in first sc, sc dec in last 2 sts, turn. (*2 sc*)

Rows 27 & 28: Rep row 24.

Row 29: Ch 1, sc dec in first 2 sts, turn. (*1 sc*)

Row 30: Ch 1, sc in sc. Fasten off.

ASSEMBLY

Referring to photo for placement, holding 2 Squares WS tog, matching ends of rows. With black, sl st tog. Fasten off.

Holding 1 long edge of 1 Corner to 1 of rem Squares, matching ends of rows and with black, sl st tog. Fasten off.

Rep with another Corner on opposite long edge of same Square.

Rep with rem Square and Corners.

With WS tog and with black, sl st Squares with Corners to top and bottom edges of the assembled 2 Squares as shown in photo.

BORDER

Rnd 1: With 1 strand of black and 1 strand of lavender held tog, join with sc in first st on top Square, sc evenly sp around rug, working 3 sc in each corner so rug will lay flat, **join** (*see Pattern Notes*) in beg sc. Fasten off lavender.

Rnd 2: With black and 1 strand of cobalt held tog, ch 1, sc in each sc around, working 2 or 3 sc in each corner so rug will lie flat and not ruffle, join in beg sc. Fasten off cobalt.

Rnd 3: With black and 1 strand of geranium held tog, rep rnd 2.

Rnd 4: With black and 1 strand of fern held tog, rep rnd 2.

Rnd 5: With black and 1 strand of light tapestry gold held tog, rep rnd 2. Fasten off all colors. ∎

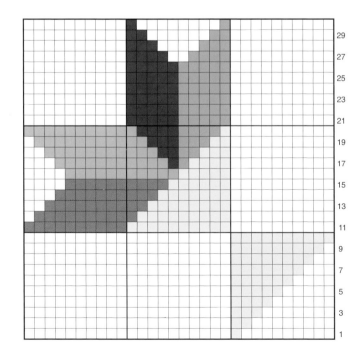

COLOR KEY
- Black
- Light Tapestry Gold
- Fern
- Cobalt
- Lavender
- Geranium

Chart

Sunflower
DESIGNS BY **TERRY DAY**
Towel Topper & Dishcloth

SKILL LEVEL

■■□□
EASY

FINISHED SIZES
Towel Topper: 12 inches x 9 inches
Dishcloth: 12 inches x 10 inches

MATERIALS
- Pisgah Yarn & Dyeing Co. Inc. Peaches & Crème medium (worsted) weight cotton yarn (2½ oz/122 yds/71g per skein): 2 skeins each #51 apple green and #1 white
- Size F/5/3.75 crochet hook or size needed to obtain gauge
- Tapestry needle
- Sewing needle
- 1 purchased dish towel
- 1-inch wooden button
- Sewing thread

GAUGE
13 hdc = 4 inches; 10 hdc rows = 4 inches

PATTERN NOTES
Weave in ends as work progresses.

Join rounds with slip stitch unless otherwise stated.

Chain-3 at beginning of row or round counts as first double crochet.

INSTRUCTIONS
TOWEL TOPPER
Row 1 (WS): With apple green, ch 58, dc in 4th ch from hook (*beg 3 sk chs count as a dc*), dc in each rem ch across, turn. (*56 dc*)

Row 2 (RS): **Ch 3** (*see Pattern Notes*), **dc dec** (*see Stitch Guide*) in next 2 dc, *****fpdc** (*see Stitch Guide*) around post of next dc, dc in next dc, rep from * across to last 3 sts, dc dec in last 3 sts, turn. (*51 sts*)

Row 3: Ch 3, *dc dec in next 2 dc, rep from * across, turn. (*27 sts*)

Row 4: Ch 3, fpdc around post of 2nd dc of next dc dec, *dc in next st, fpdc around post of 2nd dc of same dec, from * across to last 3 sts, dc dec in next 2 sts, turn, leaving beg ch-3 unworked. (*47 sts*)

Row 5: Ch 3, sk next dc, *dc dec in next 3 dc, rep from * across, turn. (*16 dc*)

Row 6: Ch 3, sk next st, [fpdc around post of first dc of next dc dec, fpdc around post of 3rd dc of same dec, fpdc around post of 2nd dc of next dc dec] 6 times, fpdc around post of first dc of next dc dec, dc in 3rd ch of beg ch-3, turn. (*21 dc*)

Row 7: Ch 3, sk next dc, [dc dec in next 3 dc] 6 times, turn, leaving beg ch-3 unworked. (*7 dc*)

Row 8: Ch 3, dc in each dc across, turn.

Rows 9–15: Rep row 8.

Row 16: Ch 3, dc in next dc, ch 3 (*buttonhole opening made*), sk next 3 dc, dc in each of last 2 dc, turn. (*4 dc, 1 ch-3 sp*)

Row 17: Ch 3, dc in each dc and in each ch across, turn. (*7 dc*)

Row 18: Ch 1, sk first dc, sc in next dc, hdc in next st, 3 dc in next st, hdc in next st, **sc dec** *(see Stitch Guide)* in last 2 sc. Fasten off.

Fold flap over to front of work. (You are at front of work when you have the tail of the yarn at end of Row 17 to your left once the flap is folded over.)

FLOWER
Rnd 1: Hold piece with front of flap facing, **join** *(see Pattern Notes)* white in any st of buttonhole opening, work 10 sc evenly sp around opening, join in beg sc.

Rnd 2: *Ch 4, sl st in next sc, rep from * around, join in joining sl st. Fasten off.

EDGING
With RS facing, join white in end of row 1,*ch 2, sl st in end of same row, ch 2, sl st in end of next row, rep from * across to end of row 7. Fasten off. Join white in opposite end of row 7, *ch 2, sl st in end of same row, ch 2, sl st in end of next row, rep from * across to end of row 7. Fasten off.

FINISHING
Cut dish towel in half, and hand- or machine-finish raw edge using sewing thread. With apple green, sew row 1 to top of dish towel, easing towel to fit size of piece. Sew button to row 10.

DISHCLOTH
Row 1 (RS): With apple green, ch 45, dc in 4th ch from hook *(beg 3 sk chs count as a dc)*, dc in each rem ch across, **changing colors** *(see stitch guide)* to white, turn. *(43 dc)*

Row 2: **Ch 3** *(see Pattern Notes)*, *fpdc *(see Stitch Guide)* around post of next dc, dc in next dc, rep from * across, turn.

Row 3: Ch 3, dc in each dc across, change to apple green, turn.

Rows 4–19: [Rep rows 2 and 3 alternately] 8 times

Row 20: Rep row 2. At end of row, do not turn.

EDGING
Ch 3, sl st in end of row 20, working down side, *ch 3, sl st in end of next row, rep from * across to next corner, working across row 1, **ch 3, sk next st, sl st in next st, rep from ** across to next corner, ch 3, working across next side, sl st in end of row, ***ch 3, sl st in end of next row, rep from *** across to next corner, working across row 20, ****ch 3, sk next st on row 20, sl st in next st, rep from **** across to beg ch-3, join in base of beg ch-3. Fasten off. ∎

Scrap Afghan

DESIGN BY **GLENDA WINKLEMAN**

SKILL LEVEL

EASY

FINISHED SIZE
51 inches x 62 inches

MATERIALS
- TLC Essentials medium (worsted) weight yarn (6 oz/312 yds/ 170g per skein):
  1 skein each #2220 butter, #2316 winter white, #2319 cherry red, #2335 taupe, #2531 light plum, #2675 dark thyme, #2680 eden green, #2772 light country rose, #2820 robin egg and #2840 medium lake blue
- Red Heart Super Saver medium (worsted) weight yarn (7 oz/364 yds/198g per skein):
  1 skein each #321 gold
- Size J/10/6mm crochet hook or size needed to obtain gauge
- Tapestry needle

GAUGE
13 sts = 4 inches; 5 rows = 4 inches

PATTERN NOTES
Weave in ends as work progresses.

Join with slip stitch unless otherwise stated.

SPECIAL STITCH
Long treble crochet (lng tr): Yo 3 times, insert hook in st indicated, yo, draw lp up to height of working row, [yo, draw through 2 lps on hook] 3 times.

INSTRUCTIONS
Row 1: With winter white, ch 159, sc in 2nd ch from hook, sc in each rem ch across, turn. *(158 sc)*

Row 2: Ch 1, working in **front lps** *(see Stitch Guide)*, sc in each sc across. Fasten off. Turn.

Row 3: Join *(see Pattern Notes)* butter in **back lp** *(see Stitch Guide)* of first sc, ch 1, sc in same lp, working in back lps, sc in each rem sc across, turn.

Row 4: Rep row 2.

Row 5: Join eden green in back lp of beg sc, ch 1, sc in back lp of each of first 2 sc, **lng tr** *(see Special Stitch)* in front lp of each of next 2 corresponding sc 3 rows below, *sk 2 sc of row 4 behind 2 tr just made, sc in back lp of each of next 6 sc, lng tr in front lp of each of next 2 corresponding sc 3 rows below, rep from * across to last 2 sc, sc in back lp of each of last 2 sc, turn.

Row 6: Ch 1, working in front lps, sc in each st across. Fasten off. Turn.

Row 7: Join medium lake blue in back lp of first sc, ch 1, sc in back lp of each of first 6 sts, *lng tr in front lp of each of next 2 corresponding sc 3 rows below, *sk 2 sc on row 6 behind 2 tr just made, sc in back lp of each of next 6 sc, rep from * across, turn.

Row 8: Ch 1, working in front lps, sc in each st across. Fasten off. Turn.

Rows 9 & 10: With light plum, rep rows 5 and 6.

Rows 11 & 12: With cherry red, rep rows 7 and 8.

Rows 13 & 14: With gold, rep rows 5 and 6.

Rows 15 & 16: With light country rose, rep rows 7 and 8.

Rows 17 & 18: With robin egg, rep rows 5 and 6.

Rows 19 & 20: With taupe, rep rows 7 and 8.

Rows 21 & 22: With dark thyme, rep rows 5 and 6.

Rows 23 & 24: With winter white, rep rows 7 and 8.

Rows 25 & 26: With butter, rep rows 5 and 6.

Rows 27 & 28: With eden green, rep rows 7 and 8.

Rows 29 & 30: With medium lake blue, rep rows 5 and 6.

Rows 31 & 32: With light plum, rep rows 7 and 8.

Rows 33 & 34: With cherry red, rep rows 5 and 6.

Rows 35 & 36: With gold, rep rows 7 and 8.

Rows 37 & 38: With light country rose, rep rows 5 and 6.

Rows 39 & 40: With robin egg, rep rows 7 and 8.

Rows 41 & 42: With taupe, rep rows 5 and 6.

Rows 43 & 44: With dark thyme, rep rows 7 and 8.

Rows 45 & 46: With winter white, rep rows 5 and 6.

Rows 47 & 48: With butter, rep rows 7 and 8.

Rows 49 & 50: With eden green, rep rows 5 and 6.

Rows 51 & 52: With medium lake blue, rep rows 7 and 8.

Rows 53 & 54: With light plum, rep rows 5 and 6.

Rows 55 & 56: With cherry red, rep rows 7 and 8.

Rows 57 & 58: With gold, rep rows 5 and 6.

Rows 59 & 60: With light country rose, rep rows 7 and 8.

Rows 61 & 62: With robin egg, rep rows 5 and 6.

Rows 63 & 64: With taupe, rep rows 7 and 8.

Rows 65 & 66: With dark thyme, rep rows 5 and 6.

Rows 67–154: [Rep rows 23–66 consecutively] twice.

Rows 155–176: Rep rows 23–44. At end of last row, fasten off.

BORDER

Holding afghan with RS facing, join medium lake blue in top right-hand corner st, ch 1, sc in each sc across to next corner st, ch 2 *(corner made)*, working across next side, sc in end of each row to next corner, ch 2 *(corner made)*, working across next side in unused lps of foundation ch, sc in each lp across to next corner, ch 2 *(corner made)*, working across next side, sc in end of each row to next corner, ch 2 *(corner made)*, join in beg sc. Fasten off. ■

Ribbon Pillow

DESIGN BY **LESHIA TWEDDLE**

SKILL LEVEL

EASY

FINISHED SIZE
18 inches x 14 inches

MATERIALS
- Medium (worsted) weight yarn: 4½ oz/210 yds/120g various types and colors
- Size I/9/5.5mm crochet hook or size needed to obtain gauge
- Size N/13/9 crochet hook
- Tapestry needle
- 12-inch x 16-inch pillow form
- Scrap ribbon (optional)

GAUGE
Size I hook: 7 sts = 4 inches; 6 rows = 4 inches

PATTERN NOTES
The pillow body is made with medium (worsted) weight yarn, changing colors as desired.

Chain-4 at beginning of row counts as first double crochet and chain-1 space.

Weave in ends as work progresses.

Join with slip stitch unless otherwise stated.

INSTRUCTIONS
BODY
Row 1: With size I hook and yarn, ch 59, dc in 6th ch from hook, [ch 1, sk next ch, dc in next ch] 26 times, dc in last ch, turn. *(27 ch-1 sps)*

Row 2: Ch 4 *(see Pattern Notes)*, sk next dc, dc in next ch-1 sp, [ch 1, sk next dc, dc in next ch-1 sp] 25 times, ch 1, 2 dc in last ch-1 sp, turn.

Rows 3–36: Rep row 2. At end of last row, fasten off, leaving long end for sewing.

STRIPS
MAKE 36.
Note: Yarn and/or ribbon can be used for strips.

For yarn strip, with size I hook, make a chain to measure 27 inches long. Fasten off.

Optional: For ribbon strip, cut ribbon to measure 27 inches.

FINISHING
With size N hook, weave Strips in ch-1 sps by going over one dc, then under the next dc, and so on, across each row.

Wrap Body around pillow form, then, using tapestry needle and end left for sewing, sew beginning row to last row.

To secure sides and create fringe, select opposite strands from each side of Body, insert and knot together. Repeat across both sides of pillow. Add additional fringe if desired. ∎

Carry-All Bag

DESIGN BY JENNY KING

SKILL LEVEL

INTERMEDIATE

FINISHED SIZE
12 inches deep x 20 inches in circumference

MATERIALS
- J. & P. Coats Royale Fashion Crochet size 3 crochet cotton (150 yds per ball):
  1 ball #325 tangerine
- Size D/3.25/3mm crochet hook or size needed to obtain gauge
- Tapestry needle

GAUGE
8 sts = 1 inch

PATTERN NOTES
Weave in ends as work progresses.

Join with slip stitch unless otherwise stated.

Chain-3 at beginning of round counts as first double crochet.

SPECIAL STITCHES
Lover knot: Pull up long lp on hook to measure ¾ inch, yo, pull through long lp, sc in back strand of long lp.

Long single crochet (lng sc): Insert hook in indicated st, draw lp up to height of love knot, yo, draw through 2 lps on hook, ch 1.

INSTRUCTIONS
BAG
Rnd 1: Ch 4, 11 dc in 4th ch from hook *(beg 3 sk chs count as a dc)*, **join** *(see Pattern Notes)* in 3rd ch of beg ch-3. *(12 dc)*

Rnd 2: **Ch 3** *(see Pattern Notes)*, dc in same ch as joining, 2 dc in each rem dc, join in 3rd ch of beg ch-3. *(24 dc)*

Rnd 3: Ch 3, dc in same ch as joining, dc in next dc, *2 dc in next dc, tr in next dc, rep from * around, join in 3rd ch of beg ch-3. *(36 sts)*

Rnd 4: Ch 3, dc in same ch as joining, dc in each of next 2 sts, *2 dc in next st, tr in each of next 2 sts, rep from * around, join in 3rd ch of beg ch-3. *(48 sts)*

Rnd 5: [2 **love knots** *(see Special Stitches)*, sk next dc, sc in next st] 23 times, love knot, **lng tsc** *(see Special Stitches)* in first st. *(47 love knots, 1 lng tsc)*

Rnd 6: [2 love knots, sk next love knot, sc in sc in center of next 2 love knots] 23 times, love knot, lng tsc in first st. *(24 love knots, 24 lng sc)]*

Rnds 7–20: Rep rnd 6.

Rnd 21: *[Love knot, sk next 2 love knots, sc in next sc] 6 times, 12 love knots, sk next 12 love knots, sc in next sc, rep from * around.

Note: Following rnds are worked in continuous rnds. Do not join; mark beg of rnds.

Rnd 22: *Love knot, sc in next sc, rep from * around.

Rnds 23–25: Rep rnd 22. Fasten off. ∎

Dishbottle Apron

DESIGN BY **TAMMY HILDEBRAND**

SKILL LEVEL

EASY

FINISHED SIZE
9 inches tall to fit standard-size dish detergent bottle

MATERIALS
- Medium (worsted) weight yarn: 2 oz/100 yds/56g assorted colors
- Size I/9/5.5mm crochet hook or size needed to obtain gauge
- Tapestry needle
- Sewing needle
- 7/16-inch button
- Sewing thread

4 MEDIUM

GAUGE
3 dc = 1 inch

PATTERN NOTES
Weave in ends as work progresses.

Join rounds with slip stitch unless otherwise stated.

Chain-3 at beginning of row counts as first double crochet.

INSTRUCTIONS
APRON
SKIRT
Note: Skirt is worked in back lps (see Stitch Guide) unless otherwise stated.

Row 1 (RS): Beg at waist with any color, ch 21, sc in 2nd ch from hook, sc in each rem ch across, ch 3, sl st over side of last sc made (*button lp made*). Fasten off. (*20 sc*)

Row 2: With RS facing, **join** (*see Pattern Notes*) any color in first sc, ch 1, 2 sc in same sc, sc in each of next 9 sc, 2 sc in next sc, sc in each rem sc across. Fasten off. (*22 sc*)

Rnd 3: Now working in rnds, with RS facing, join any color in first sc, ch 1, 2 sc in same st, sc in each rem sc around, working 2 sc in center sc, join in beg sc. Fasten off. (*24 sc*)

Rnds 4–24: Rep rnd 3. (*66 sc at end of last rnd*)

BIB
Row 1: With RS facing, sk first 6 unused lps at bottom of foundation ch, join any color in next unused lp, **ch 3** (*see Pattern Notes*), dc in each of next 7 unused lps. Fasten off, leaving rem unused lps unworked. (*8 dc*)

Row 2: With RS facing, join any color in 3rd ch of beg ch-3, ch 3, dc in each rem dc across. Fasten off.

Rows 3 & 4: Rep row 2.

Row 5: With RS facing, join any color in 3rd ch of beg ch-3, ch 3, dc in each rem dc across, ch 12, turn, join in 3rd ch of beg ch-3. Fasten off.

BIB EDGING

With RS facing, join any color in first unused lp of foundation ch of Skirt to right of first st of row 1 of Bib, ch 1, sc in same st, ch 3, working in ends of rows up side of Bib, [sc, ch 3] twice in end of each row, [sc in next ch, ch 3] 12 times, working down next side of Bib, [sc, ch 3] twice in end of each row to waist, sc in next unused lp on foundation ch. Fasten off.

SKIRT RUFFLES
FIRST RUFFLE

With RS facing, join same color as used for row 2 of Skirt in first unused lp of first sc on row 2 at back opening, ch 1, sc in same lp, *ch 3, sc in next unused lp, rep from * across. Fasten off.

2ND RUFFLE

Sk next 2 rnds on Skirt, join same color as used for next rnd in first unused lp of rnd at back opening, ch 1, sc in same lp, ch 3, *sc in next unused lp, ch 3, rep from * around, join in beg sc.

3RD THROUGH 8TH RUFFLES

Work same as 2nd Ruffle.

FINISHING

Sew button to row 1 of Skirt opposite button lp. ∎

Hot Pads

DESIGNS BY **LOUISE PUCHATY**

SKILL LEVEL

EASY

FINISHED SIZE

5½ inches x 5½ inches

MATERIALS

- Medium (worsted) weight cotton yarn:
    70 yds MC
- Size 10 crochet cotton:
    18 yds CC
    2½ yds yellow
- Size G/6/4mm crochet hook or size needed to botain guage
- Size 6/1.8mm steel crochet hook
- Sewing needle
- Tapestry needle
- ¾-inch plastic ring
- Sewing thread

GAUGE
Size G hook: Rnds 1–9 = 2 inches

PATTERN NOTES
Weave in ends as work progresses.

Join with slip stitch unless otherwise stated.

Chain-3 at beginning of row or round count as a first double crochet.

SPECIAL STITCH
Cluster (cl): Holding back last lp of each tr on hook, 2 tr in indicated sp, yo, draw through all 3 lps on hook.

INSTRUCTIONS
Note: Hot pad is worked in continuous rnds. Do not join unless specified; mark beg of rnds.

HOT PAD
Rnd 1 (RS): With size G hook and MC, ch 22, sc in 2nd ch from hook, sc in each rem ch across, working in unused lps on opposite side of foundation ch, sc in each lp around. *(42 sc)*

Rnd 2: Sc in each sc around.

Rnds 3–23: Rep rnd 2. At end of last rnd, fasten off, leaving 8-inch end.

HANGING RING
Join MC with sc in plastic ring, 13 sc in ring, **join** *(see Pattern Notes)* in joining sc.

FLOWER
Rnd 1 (RS): With size 6 steel hook and yellow, ch 6, join in first ch to form ring, ch 1, sc in ring, ch 4, *cl *(see Special Stitch)* in ring, ch 4 **, sc in ring, ch 4, rep from * 6 times, ending last rep at **, join in beg sc.

Rnd 2: Working behind cl, [ch 4, sl st in next sc] 5 times, ch 4, join in joining sl st. Fasten off.

FIRST PETAL
Row 1: With size 6 steel hook, join CC in any ch-4 sp on rnd 1, **ch 3** *(see Pattern Notes)*, 8 dc in same sp, ch 1, turn. *(9 dc)*

Row 2: Ch 1, 2 sc in first dc, sc in each of next 7 dc, 2 sc in 3rd ch of beg ch-3, turn. *(11 dc)*

Row 3: Ch 1, sc in each sc, turn.

Rows 4 & 5: Rep row 3.

Row 6: Ch 1, **sc dec** *(see Stitch Guide)* in first 2 sc, sc in each of next 7 dc, sc dec in last 2 sc, turn. *(9 sc)*

Row 7: Ch 1, sc in each sc across, turn.

Row 8: Ch 1, sc dec in first 2 sc, sc in each of next 5 dc, sc dec in last 2 sc, turn. *(7 sc)*

Row 9: Ch 1, sc in each sc across, turn.

Row 10: Ch 1, sc dec in first 2 sc, sc in each of next 3 dc, sc dec in last 2 sc, turn. *(5 sc)*

Row 11: Rep row 9.

Row 12: Ch 1, sc dec in first 2 sc, sc in next dc, sc dec in last 2 sc, turn. *(3 sc)*

Row 13: Ch 1, sc dec in 3 sc. Fasten off.

2ND THROUGH 5TH PETALS
Work same as First Petal in each rem ch-4 sp.

FINISHING
Sew Flower to center of Hot Pad. Sew Hot Pad closed by picking up outside lp of each sc. Sew Hanging Ring to 1 corner. ■

Daffodil
Tea Cozy & Coasters

DESIGNS BY **LISA MARCHAND HARRIS**

SKILL LEVEL

EASY

FINISHED SIZE
Fits a medium-size tea pot (4 cups)

MATERIALS
- Bernat Super Value medium (worsted) weight yarn (7 oz/ 382 yds/197g per ball):
  1 ball each #53244 forest green, #07414 natural and #00608 bright yellow
- Bernat Satin medium (worsted) weight yarn (3½ oz/163 yds/100g per ball):
  1 ball each #04236 evergreen and #04615 banana
- Size H/8/5mm crochet hook or size needed to obtain gauge
- Size E/4/3.5mm crochet hook
- Tapestry needle

4 MEDIUM

GAUGE
13 hdc = 4 inches; 10 hdc rows = 4 inches

PATTERN NOTES
Weave in ends as work progresses.

Join rounds with slip stitch unless otherwise stated.

Chain-2 at beginning of row or round counts as first half double crochet.

Chain-3 at beginning of row or round counts as first double crochet.

INSTRUCTIONS
COZY
Row 1 (RS): With size H hook and natural, leaving a 10-inch length, ch 33, hdc in 3rd ch

from hook (*beg 2 sk chs count as a hdc*), hdc in each rem ch, turn. (*32 hdc*)

Row 2: **Ch 2** (*see Pattern Notes*), working in **back lps** (*see Stitch Guide*), hdc in each st across, turn.

Rows 3 & 4: Rep row 2. At end of last row, **changing colors** (*see Stitch Guide*) to forest green.

Rows 5 & 6: Rep row 2. At end of last row, change to natural.

Rows 7–10: Rep row 2. At end of last row, change to forest green.

Rows 11 & 12: Rep row 2. At end of last row, change to natural.

Rows 13–16: Rep row 2. At end of last row, change to forest green.

Row 17: Working in back lps, hdc in each of next 10 hdc, ch 9 (*spout opening made*), sk next 9 hdc, hdc in each rem hdc across, turn.

Row 18: Ch 2, working in back lps, hdc in each hdc and in each ch across, turn. Change to natural.

Rows 19–22: Rep row 2. At end of last row, change to forest green.

Rows 23 & 24: Rep row 2. At end of last row, change to natural.

Rows 25–28: Rep row 2. At end of last row, change to forest green.

Rows 29 & 30: Rep row 2. At end of last row, change to natural.

Rows 31–34: Rep row 2. At end of last row, change to forest green .

Rows 35 & 36: Rep row 2. At end of last row, fasten off.

ASSEMBLY
With WS facing, sew first 6 sts of row 38 to first 6 sts of row 1. Sew last 9 sts of row 38 to last 9 sts of row 1 to form opening for handle.

TIE
With size H hook and natural, ch 50, fasten off. Weave through sts at top of Cozy to tighten and close top. Tie on inside of Cozy so Tie does not show on outside.

DAFFODIL
HEAD
Rnd 1: With size E hook and banana, ch 4, **join** *(see Pattern Notes)* in first ch to form ring, **ch 3** *(see Pattern Notes)*, 11 dc in ring, join in 3rd ch of beg ch-3. *(12 dc)*

Rnd 2: Ch 3, working in back lps, dc in each dc around, join in 3rd ch of beg ch-3.

Rnd 3: Ch 3, dc in each dc, join in 3rd ch of beg ch-3.

Rnd 4: Ch 1, sc in same ch as joining, ch 2, *sc in next dc, ch 2, rep from * around in beg sc. Fasten off. *(12 sc, 12 ch-2 sps)*

Rnd 5: Join bright yellow with sc in unused **front lp** *(see Stitch Guide)* of any st on rnd 1, ch 2, working in rem unused front lps, sk next lp, *sc in next lp, ch 2, sk next lp, rep from * around, join in beg sc. *(6 ch-2 sps)*

Rnd 6: Sl st in next ch-2 sp, *ch 2, (tr, 3 dtr, tr, ch 2, sc) in same sp *(petal made)*, sl st in next ch-2 sp, rep from * around, join in beg sl st. *(6 petals)*

Rnd 7: *2 sc in next ch-2 sp, sc in each of next 2 sts, (sc, ch 4, sl st in 3rd ch from hook, sc) in next st, sc in each of next 2 sc, 2 sc in next ch-2 sp, rep from * around, join in beg sc. Fasten off.

Rnd 8: Working behind petals, join evergreen with **fpsc** *(see Stitch Guide)* around post of any st on rnd 5, ch 4, sk next st, *fpsc around post of next st, ch 4, sk next, rep from * around, join in beg sc.

Rnd 9: Sl st in next ch-4 sp, *ch 2, (tr, 3 dtr, tr, ch 2, sc) in same sp *(petal made)*, sl st in next ch-4 sp, rep from * around, join in beg sl st. Turn. *(6 petals)*

Rnd 10: Ch 1, *hdc in next ch-2 sp, hdc in each of next 2 sts, 3 hdc in next st, hdc in each of next 2 sts, hdc in next ch-2 sp, rep from * around, join in beg hdc. Turn.

Rnd 11: Ch 1, sc in same hdc, sc in each of next 3 sts, *(sc, ch 3, sl st in 3rd ch from hook, sc) in next st **, sc in each of next 8 sts, rep from * around, ending last rep at **, sc in each of next 4 sts, join in beg sc. Fasten off.

LEAVES
MAKE 3.

With size E hook and evergreen, ch 8, sc in 2nd ch from hook, hdc in each of next 2 chs, 2 dc in next ch, hdc in each of next 2 chs, 4 sc in last ch, working in unused lps on opposite side of ch, sc in each lp across, join in beg sc. Fasten off.

STEM

With size E hook and evergreen, ch 30. Fasten off.

FINISHING

Referring to photo for placement, sew Daffodil Head, Stem and Leaves to Cozy. Sew around outside of all Leaves (including Leaves on back of the Head) and Stem.

Cut 24-inch strand of natural and weave around bottom of Cozy. Tie after inserting tea pot.

COASTERS
SKILL LEVEL

EASY

FINISHED SIZE

5 inches in diameter

MATERIALS

- Bernat Super Value medium (worsted) weight yarn (7 oz/ 382 yds/197g per skein): 1 skein each #53244 forest green, #07414 natural and #07445 yellow
- Size H/8/5mm crochet hook or size needed to obtain gauge
- Tapestry needle

4 MEDIUM

GAUGE

13 hdc = 4 inches; 10 hdc rows = 4 inches

PATTERN NOTES

Weave in ends as work progresses.

Join rounds with slip stitch unless otherwise stated.

Chain-3 at beginning of round counts as first double crochet.

SPECIAL STITCHES

Beginning shell (beg shell): Ch 3, 2 dc in place indicated.

Shell: 3 dc in sp indicated.

INSTRUCTIONS
COASTER

Rnd 1 (RS): With yellow, ch 4, **join** (see Pattern Notes) in first ch to form ring, **ch 3** (see Pattern Notes), 11 dc in ring, join in 3rd ch of beg ch-3. (12 dc)

Rnd 2: **Beg shell** (see Special Stitches) in same ch as joining, ch 1, sk next st, [**shell** (see Special Stitches) in next st, ch 1, sk next st] 5 times, join in 3rd ch of beg ch-3. Fasten off. (6 shells, 6 ch-1 sps)

Rnd 3: Join forest green in any ch-1 sp, beg shell in same sp, ch 1, sk next st, dc in next st, ch 1, sk next, *shell in next ch-1 sp, ch 1, sk next st, dc in next st, ch 1, sk next st, rep from * around, join in 3rd ch of beg ch-3. Fasten off. (6 shells, 6 dc, 12 ch-1 sps)

Rnd 4: Join natural in 2nd dc of any shell, beg shell in same st, shell in each of next 2 ch-1 sps **, shell in 2nd dc of next shell, rep from * around, ending last rep at **, join in 3rd ch of beg ch-3. Fasten off. (18 shells)

Rnd 5: Join forest green in any dc, ch 1, sc in same dc, sc in each rem dc around, join in beg sc. Fasten off. (54 sc) ■

Trio of Trivets

DESIGNS BY **RHONDA DODDS**

SKILL LEVEL

INTERMEDIATE

FINISHED SIZES

Sunflower: 10½ inches in diameter
Pumpkin: 8½ inches in diameter
Watermelon: 9 inches x 11½ inches

MATERIALS
Sunflower:
- Medium (worsted) weight cotton yarn:
  3 oz/150 yds/84g each medium brown, dark brown, cornmeal and gold
- Size J/10/6mm crochet hook or size needed to obtain gauge
- Tapestry needle
- Sunflower button (optional)

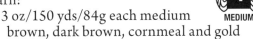

Pumpkin:
- Medium (worsted) weight cotton yarn:
  3 oz/150 yds/84g each burnt orange, green and medium brown
- Size I/9/5.5mm crochet hook or size needed to obtain gauge
- Tapestry needle
- Stitch marker

Watermelon:
- Medium (worsted) weight cotton yarn:
  3 oz/150 yds/84g each red, white, green, dark green and black
- Size H/8/5mm crochet hook or size needed to obtain gauge
- Tapestry needle
- Watermelon button (optional)

GAUGE
With size J hook and 2 strands held tog: 13 sts = 4 inches; 5 rows = 4 inches

PATTERN NOTES
Weave in ends as work progresses.

Join with slip stitch unless otherwise stated.

Chain-3 at beginning of row or round counts as first double crochet.

SPECIAL STITCHES
Beginning shell (beg shell): Ch 3, 4 dc in sp indicated.
Shell: 5 dc in sp indicated.

INSTRUCTIONS
SUNFLOWER

Rnd 1: With size J hook and 1 strand of medium brown and 1 strand of dark brown held tog, ch 4, **join** (*see Pattern Notes*) in first ch to form ring, **ch 3** (*see Pattern Notes*), 11 dc in ring, join in 3rd ch of beg ch-3. (*12 dc*)

Rnd 2: Ch 3, dc in same ch as joining, 2 dc in each dc around, join in 3rd ch of beg ch-3. (*24 dc*)

Rnd 3: Ch 3, 2 dc in next dc, *dc in next dc, 2 dc in next dc, rep from * around, join in 3rd ch of beg ch-3. (*36 dc*)

Rnd 4: Ch 3, dc in next dc, 2 dc in next dc, *dc in each of next 2 dc, 2 dc in next dc, rep from * around, join in 3rd ch of beg ch-3. Fasten off. (*48 dc*)

Rnd 5: Join cornmeal in any dc, ch 1, sc in same dc, sc in next dc, 2 sc in next dc, *sc in each of next 2 dc, 2 sc in next dc, rep from * around, join in beg sc. (*66 sc*)

Rnd 6: **Beg shell** (*see Special Stitches*) in same ch as joining, sk next sc, dc in next sc, sk next sc,* **shell** (*see Special Stitches*) in next sc, sk next sc, dc in next sc, rep from * around, join in 3rd ch of beg ch-3. Fasten off. (*16 shells, 16 dc*)

Rnd 7: Join gold in same ch as joining of rnd 6, ch 1, sc in same ch, sc in next dc, *3 dc in next dc, sc in each of next 5 dc, rep from * 14 times, 3 dc in next dc, sc in each of last 3 dc, join in beg sc. (*48 dc, 80 sc*) Turn.

HANGING LOOP

Ch 8, sl st in same sc as last joining sl st made, ch 1, turn, sc in each ch around, sl st in same sp as last joining sl st. Fasten off.

FINISHING

Referring to photo for placement, sew button to Sunflower.

PUMPKIN

Rnd 1: With size I hook and burnt orange, ch 4, **join** (*see Pattern Notes*) in first ch to form ring, **ch 3** (*see Pattern Notes*), 11 dc in ring, join in 3rd ch of beg ch-3. (*12 dc*)

Rnd 2: Ch 3, dc in same ch as joining, 2 dc in each dc around, join in 3rd ch of beg ch-3. (*24 dc*)

Rnd 3: Ch 3, 2 dc in next dc, *dc in next dc, 2 dc in next dc, rep from * around, join in 3rd ch of beg ch-3. (*36 dc*)

Rnd 4: Ch 3, dc in next dc, 2 dc in next dc, *dc in each of next 2 dc, 2 dc in next dc, rep from * around, join in 3rd ch of beg ch-3. Fasten off. (*48 dc*)

Rnd 5: Ch 3, dc in each of next 2 dc, 2 dc in next dc, *dc in each of next 3 dc, 2 dc in next dc, rep from *around, join in 3rd ch of beg ch-3. (*60 dc*)

Rnd 6: Ch 1, sc in same ch as joining, sc in next dc, [hdc in next dc, dc in each of next 2 dc, hdc in next dc, sc in each of next 2 dc] twice, hdc in next dc, dc in each of next 2 dc, hdc in next dc, sc in each of next 22 dc (*mark last sc made*), sc in each rem dc, join in beg sc. Fasten off.

STEM

Row 1: Join 2 strands of medium brown in marked sc, ch 1, sc in same sc, sc in each of next 6 sc, turn, leaving rem sts unworked. (*7 sc*)

Row 2: Ch 3, dc in each sc across, turn.

Row 3: Ch 3, dc in each dc across, turn.

Row 4: Ch 4, dc in next dc, sc in each of next 2 dc, hdc in next dc, dc in next dc, tr in last dc. Fasten off.

LEAF
MAKE 2.

With 2 strands of green held tog, ch 9, sc in 2nd ch from hook, sc in each of next 2 chs, hdc in next ch, dc in each of next 3 chs, 7 dc in last ch, working in unused lps on opposite side of foundation ch, dc in each of next 3 lps, hdc in next lp, sc in each of next 2 lps, join in beg sc. Fasten off.

FINISHING
Referring to photo for placement, sew Leaves to front of Pumpkin.

WATERMELON
Row 1: With size H hook and 2 strands of dark green held tog, ch 31, dc in 4th ch from hook *(beg 3 sk chs count as a dc)*, dc in each rem ch across, turn. *(28 dc)*

Row 2: **Ch 3** *(see Pattern Notes)*, dc in each dc across. Fasten off.

Row 3: **Join** *(see Pattern Notes)*, 2 strands of green in last dc made, ch 2, hdc in same dc, hdc in each rem dc across. Fasten off.

Row 4: Join 1 strand of white in last hdc made, ch 1, sc in same hdc, sc in each rem hdc across. Fasten off.

Row 5: Join 1 strand of red in last sc made, ch 3, dc in each dc across, turn.

Row 6: Ch 3, dc in each dc across, turn.

Row 7: Ch 3, **dc dec** *(see Stitch Guide)* in next 2 sts, dc in each of next 22 dc, dc dec in next 2 sts, dc in last dc, turn. *(26 dc)*

Row 8: Ch 3, dc dec in next 2 sts, dc in each of next 20 dc, dc dec in next 2 sts, dc in last dc, turn. *(24 dc)*

Row 9: Ch 3, dc dec in next 2 sts, dc in each of next 18 dc, dc dec in next 2 sts, dc in last dc, turn. *(22 dc)*

Row 10: Ch 3, dc dec in next 2 sts, dc in each of next 16 dc, dc dec in next 2 sts, dc in last dc, turn. *(20 dc)*

Row 11: Ch 3, dc dec in next 2 sts, dc in each of next 14 dc, dc dec in next 2 sts, dc in last dc, turn. *(18 dc)*

Row 12: Ch 3, dc dec in next 2 sts, dc in each of next 12 dc, dc dec in next 2 sts, dc in last dc, turn. *(16 dc)*

Row 13: Ch 3, dc dec in next 2 sts, dc in each of next 10 dc, dc dec in next 2 sts, dc in last dc, turn. *(14 dc)*

Row 14: Ch 3, dc dec in next 2 sts, dc in each of next 8 dc, dc dec in next 2 sts, dc in last dc, turn. *(12 dc)*

Row 15: Ch 3, dc dec in next 2 sts, dc in each of next 6 dc, dc dec in next 2 sts, dc in last dc, turn. *(10 dc)*

Row 16: Ch 3, dc dec in next 2 sts, dc in each of next 4 dc, dc dec in next 2 sts, dc in last dc, turn. *(8 dc)*

Row 17: Ch 3, dc dec in next 2 sts, dc in each of next 4 dc, dc dec in next 2 sts, dc in last dc, turn. *(6 dc)*

Row 18: Ch 3, dc in next 4 sts, dc in last dc, turn. *(3 sts)*

LOOP
Ch 9, join in top of last st made, ch 1, turn, sc in each ch, sl st in same sp as joining sl st. Fasten off.

TRIM
Hold piece with RS facing, join dark green in bottom right corner, ch 1, 2 sc in same sp, sc evenly sp to next corner, 3 sc in corner, sc evenly sp to beg sc, join in beg sc. Fasten off.

SEED
MAKE 6.
Note: Hide ends within seed to make seeds look fuller.

With 1 strand of black, ch 4, 2 dc in 4th ch from hook, drop lp from hook, insert hook in top of ch-4, then insert hook in dc just made and draw through lp on hook. Fasten off.

FINISHING
Referring to photo for placement, sew Seeds to Watermelon. ∎

Glass Cozies

DESIGNS BY **ELLEN GORMLEY**

SKILL LEVEL

EASY

FINISHED SIZES

Juice Glass Cozy: 3½ inches x 2½ inches
High Ball Glass Cozy: 2½ inches x 4 inches

MATERIALS

- Lily Sugar'n Cream medium (worsted) weight cotton yarn (2½ oz/120 yds/71g per ball): 1 ball #00026 light blue
- Size H/8/5mm crochet hook or size needed to obtain gauge
- Tapestry needle

4 MEDIUM

GAUGE

3 hdc = 1 inch

PATTERN NOTES

Weave in ends as work progresses.

Join rounds with slip stitch unless otherwise stated.

Chain-2 at beginning of round counts as first half double crochet.

Chain-3 at beginning of round counts as first double crochet.

INSTRUCTIONS
JUICE GLASS COZY

Note: Cozy is worked in continuous rnds. Do not join unless specified; mark beginning of rnds.

Rnd 1: Ch 8, **join** (see Pattern Notes) in first ch to form ring, ch 1, 2 sc in each ch. (16 sc)

Rnd 2: [Sc in next sc, 2 sc in next sc] 8 times. (24 sc)

Rnd 3: Working in **back lps** (see Stitch Guide), sc in each sc.

Rnd 4: Sl st in next sc, **ch 3** (see Pattern Notes), dc in each rem sc, join in 3rd ch of beg ch-3.

Rnd 5: Ch 2 *(see Pattern Notes)*, hdc in each of next 2 sts, **fpdc** *(see Stitch Guide)* around next st, [hdc in each of next 3 sts, fpdc around next st] 4 times, join in 2nd ch of beg ch-2.

Rnds 6–11: Rep rnd 5. At end of last rnd, fasten off.

HIGH BALL GLASS COZY

Note: Cozy is worked in continuous rnds. Do not join unless specified; mark beginning of rnds.

Rnd 1: Ch 8, **join** *(see Pattern Notes)* in first ch to form ring, ch 1, 2 sc in each ch. *(16 sc)*

Rnd 2: [Sc in next sc, 2 sc in next sc] 8 times. *(24 sc)*

Rnd 3: [Sc in each of next 2 sc, 2 sc in next sc] 8 times. *(32 sc)*

Rnd 4: [Sc in each of next 3 sc, 2 sc in next sc] 8 times, join in next sc. *(40 sc)*

Rnd 5: Ch 3 *(see Pattern Notes)*, working in **back lps** *(see Stitch Guide)*, dc in each of next 39 sc, join in 3rd ch of beg ch-3.

Rnd 6: Ch 2 *(see Pattern Notes)*, **fpdc** *(see Stitch Guide)* around next st, [hdc in next dc, fpdc around next st] 19 times, join in 2nd ch of beg ch-2. *(20 hdc, 20 fpdc)*

Rnd 7: Ch 2, *sk next fpdc, sk hdc, fpdc around next fpdc, hdc in sk hdc, fpdc around sk fpdc, hdc in next hdc, rep from * 8 times, sk next fpdc, sk next hdc, fpdc around next fpdc, hdc in sk hdc, fpdc around sk fpdc, join in 2nd ch of beg ch-2.

Rnd 8: Ch 2, fpdc around next fpdc, [hdc in next hdc, fpdc around next fpdc] 19 times, join in 2nd ch of beg ch-2.

Rnds 9 & 10: Rep rnds 7 and 8. At end of rnd 10, fasten off. ∎

Table Runner

DESIGN BY **MARTY MILLER**

SKILL LEVEL

■□□□
EASY

FINISHED SIZE
16 inches x 32 inches

MATERIALS
- Pisgah Yarn & Dyeing Co. Inc. Peaches & Crème medium (worsted) weight cotton yarn (solids: 2½ oz/122 yds/71g per ball; ombres: 2 oz/98 yds/57g per ball): 1 ball each #1 white and #165 daisy ombre
- Size I/9/5.5mm crochet hook or size needed to obtain gauge
- Tapestry needle

4 MEDIUM

GAUGE
20 sc = 4 inches; 16 sc rows = 4 inches

PATTERN NOTES
Weave in ends as work progresses.

Two ways to start the table runner are given. Method 1 uses the foundation chain as usual. Method 2 uses the single crochet foundation stitch. Use whichever method you like.

Join with slip stitch unless otherwise stated.

Work the following color sequence: *White, white, daisy ombre, rep from * for 63 rows. Work 2 rows with white to finish.

SPECIAL STITCHES

Beginning single crochet foundation st (beg sc foundation st): Ch 2, insert hook in 2nd ch from hook, yo, draw lp through, yo, draw through 1 lp on hook (*base ch completed*), yo, draw through 2 lps on hook.

Single crochet foundation st (sc foundation st): *Insert hook in last base ch completed, yo, draw lp through, yo, draw through 1 lp on hook (*base ch*), yo, draw through 2 lps on hook, rep from * until desired number of sts have been completed. (*The ch-2 at beg of row does NOT count as a sc foundation st.*)

INSTRUCTIONS

METHOD 1

Foundation row: With white and leaving 10-inch end, ch 167, sc in 2nd ch from hook, sc in each rem ch across, turn. (*166 sc*)

Beg with row 1 following Method 2 foundation row.

METHOD 2

Foundation row: With white and leaving 10-inch end, work **beg sc foundation st** (*see Special Stitches*), work **sc foundation st** (*see Special Stitches*) 165 times, turn. (*166 sc*)

Row 1: Ch 1, sc in first st, *ch 1, sk next st, sc in next st, rep from * across to last 2 sts, sc in each of last 2 sts. Fasten off, leaving 10-inch end. Turn. (*83 sc*)

Row 2: Leaving a 10-inch end, **join** (*see Pattern Notes*) daisy ombre in first sc, ch 1, sc in same sc, *ch 1, sk next sc, sc in next ch-1 sp, rep from * across to last ch-1 sp, sc in last ch-1 sp, sc in last sc. Fasten off, leaving 10-inch end. Turn.

Row 4: Leaving 10-inch end, join white in first sc, ch 1, sc in same sc, *ch 1, sk next sc, sc in next ch-1 sp, rep from * across to last ch-1 sp, sc in last ch-1 sp, sc in last sc.

Row 5: Ch 1, sc in first sc, *ch 1, sk next sc, sc in next ch-1 sp, rep from * across to last ch-1 sp, sc in last ch-1 sp, sc in last sc. Fasten off, leaving 10-inch end. Turn.

Rows 6–65: [Rep rows 3–5 consecutively] 20 times. At end of last row, fasten off.

FRINGE

Cut 130 16-inch strands of each color for fringe. Use 1 strand of each color for each knot of fringe plus strand left at end of rows. Fold strands in half. Insert hook in end of first row and draw folded end through. Draw ends through fold and tighten knot. Tie knots in each row across both short ends. Trim ends even. ■

Flowerberry

DESIGN BY CHRISTINA MCMAHON

SKILL LEVEL

EASY

FINISHED SIZE

3½ inches wide x 4½ inches tall

MATERIALS

- Medium (worsted) weight feltable wool yarn:
  2 oz/100 yds/56g each pink, black and green
- Size H/8/5mm crochet hook or size needed to obtain gauge
- Tapestry needle
- Sewing needle
- ⅝-inch shank button
- Swivel clasp
- Sewing thread

4 MEDIUM

GAUGE

Gauge not important to this project.

PATTERN NOTES

Weave in ends as work progresses.

Join rounds with slip stitch unless otherwise stated.

INSTRUCTIONS

BAG

Rnd 1: With black, ch 22, sc in 2nd ch from hook, sc in each ch across to last ch, 2 sc in last ch, working in unused lps on opposite side of foundation ch, sc in each lp across, 2 sc in last ch, **join** (see Pattern Notes) in beg sc. (44 sc)

Rnd 2: Ch 1, sc in each sc, join in beg sc.

Rnds 3–10: Rep rnd 2. At end of rnd 10, fasten off.

Rnd 11: Join pink in any sc, ch 1, sc in each sc, join in beg sc. Fasten off.

Rnd 12: Join black in any sc, ch 1, sc in each sc, join in beg sc.

Rnds 13–17: Rep rnd 2. At end of rnd 17, turn.

STRAP

Row 1: Ch 1, sc in **back lp** (see Stitch Guide) of each of first 4 sts, turn, leaving rem sts unworked.

Row 2: Ch 1, sc through both lps of each sc, turn.

Rep row 2 until Strap measures 1½ inches. Fasten off

EDGING

Join pink in any st on rnd 17, ch 1, sc in each sc around, including sc used for Strap sts, join in beg sc. Fasten off.

ROSE

With pink, ch 53, dc in 4th ch from hook, dc in each rem ch across. Fasten off.

LEAF
MAKE 2.

Row 1: With green, ch 2, 2 sc in 2nd ch from hook, turn. *(2 sc)*

Row 2: Ch 1, 2 sc in each of next 2 sc, turn. *(4 sc)*

Row 3: Ch 1, 2 sc in first sc, sc in each of next 2 sc, 2 sc in last sc, turn. *(6 sc)*

Row 4: Ch 1, sc in each sc across, turn.

Row 5: Rep row 4.

Row 6: Ch 1, **sc dec** *(see Stitch Guide)* in first 2 sc, sc in each of next 2 sc, sc dec in last 2 sc, turn. *(4 sc)*

Row 7: Ch 1, sc dec in first 2 sc, sc dec in next 2 sc. Fasten off. *(2 sc)*

FINISHING

Felt all pieces and dry completely. With pink felted piece, roll up and sew bottom edges together with sewing needle and thread to form a rose. Referring to photo for placement, sew to Bag. Sew button to middle of Rose. Referring to photo for placement, sew Leaves to Bag. Place clasp on Strap, fold Strap down and sew securely. ∎

Tape Measure Covers

DESIGNS BY **FRANCES HUGHES**

SKILL LEVEL

EASY

FINISHED SIZE

Fits a 2-inch round tape measure

MATERIALS

- Size 10 crochet cotton:
    2 yds each emerald green, light green, red, yellow, and pink
- Size B/1/2.25mm crochet hook or size needed to obtain gauge
- Tapestry needle
- Purchased 2-inch round tape measure
- Petite glass beads
- Craft glue

GAUGE

Rnd 1 = ⅝ inch

PATTERN NOTES

Weave in ends as work progresses.

Join with slip stitch unless otherwise stated.

Chain-2 at beginning of round counts as first half double crochet.

Chain-3 at beginning of round counts as first double crochet.

INSTRUCTIONS
POINSETTIA COVER
FRONT/BACK
MAKE 2.

Rnd 1 (RS): With emerald green, ch 4, **join** (see *Pattern Notes*) in first ch to form ring, **ch 3** (see *Pattern Notes*), 11 dc in ring, join in 3rd ch of beg ch-3. *(12 dc)*

Rnd 2: Ch 3, dc in same ch as joining, 2 dc in each rem dc around, join in 3rd ch of beg ch-3. *(24 dc)*

Rnd 3: Ch 3, dc in same ch as joining, dc in next dc, *2 dc in next dc, dc in next dc, rep from * around, join in 3rd ch of beg ch-3. *(36 dc)*

Rnd 4: Ch 3, dc in next dc, 2 dc in next dc, *dc in each of next 2 dc, 2 dc in next dc, rep from * around, join in 3rd ch of beg ch-3. *(48 dc)*

Rnd 5: **Ch 2** (see *Pattern Notes*), hdc in each of next 45 dc. Fasten off, leaving rem 2 dc unworked. *(46 hdc)*

LEAF
MAKE 2.
With light green, ch 8, sc in 2nd ch from hook, hdc in each of next 2 chs, dc in each of next 3 chs, 7 tr in last ch, working in unused lps on opposite side of foundation ch, dc in each of next 3 lps, hdc in each of next 2 lps, sc in last lp, join in beg sc. Fasten off.

POINSETTIA
Rnd 1: With red, ch 2, 6 sc in 2nd ch from hook, join in beg sc. *(6 sc)*

Rnd 2: Ch 1, 2 sc in each sc around, join in beg ch-1. *(12 sc)*

Rnd 3: *Ch 2, (2 tr, ch 3, sl st in 3rd ch from hook, 2 tr, ch 2, sl st) in same sc (*petal made*), sl st in next sc, rep from * 10 times, ch 2, (2 tr, ch 3, sl st in 3rd ch from hook, 2 tr, ch 2, sl st)

in same sc (*petal made*), join in joining sl st. Fasten off. *(11 petals)*

FINISHING
Hold pieces with WS facing, sew tog, inserting tape measure with tape tab in opening formed by sk dc before completely closing. Referring to photo for placement, glue Poinsettia and Leaves to center of Cover. Glue beads to center of Poinsettia.

WILD ROSE COVER
FRONT/BACK
MAKE 2.
Rnds 1–5: Rep rnds 1–5 of Front/Back of Poinsettia Cover.

FLOWER
Rnd 1: With yellow, ch 2, 6 sc in 2nd ch from hook, join in beg sc. *(6 sc)*

Rnd 2: Ch 1, 2 sc in same sc, 2 sc in each rem sc around, join in beg sc. Fasten off. *(12 sc)*

Rnd 3: Join pink in any sc, ch 1, 2 sc in same sc, 2 sc in each rem sc around, join in **back lp** (see *Stitch Guide*) of beg sc. *(24 sc)*

Rnd 4: Ch 1, sc in same lp, working in back lps, sc in next sc, *(hdc, dc, 3 tr, dc, hdc) in next sc (*petal made*) **, sc in each of next 2 sc, rep from * around, ending last rep at **, join in **front lp** (see *Stitch Guide*) of beg sc. *(8 petals)*

Rnd 5: Ch 1, sc in same lp, working in front lps, sc in next sc, (hdc, 2 dc, hdc) in next st (*small petal made*), *sc in each of next 2 sc, (hdc, 2 dc, hdc) in next st, rep from * around, join in beg sc. Fasten off. *(8 small petals)*

LEAF
MAKE 3.
With light green, ch 2, (sc, hdc, dc, ch 3, sl st in 3rd ch from hook, dc, hdc, sc) in 2nd ch from hook, join in beg sc. Fasten off.

FINISHING
Hold pieces with WS facing, sew tog, inserting tape measure with tape tab in opening formed by sk dc before completely closing. Referring to photo for placement, glue Wild Rose and 2 Leaves to center of Cover. Glue 1 Leaf to tape tab. ■

Blue Wrap

DESIGN BY **RUTHIE MARKS**

SKILL LEVEL

EASY

FINISHED SIZE
11 inches wide x 50 inches (long sides)

MATERIALS
- Plymouth Encore Worsted medium (worsted) weight yarn (3½ oz/ 200 yds/100g per skein): 2 skeins each #514 light blue, #515 medium blue, #598 dark blue, #555 navy
- Size H/8/5mm crochet hook or size needed to obtain gauge
- Tapestry needle
- Stitch markers

4 MEDIUM

GAUGE
5 dc/4 ch-1 sps = 2½ inches

PATTERN NOTES
Weave in ends as work progresses.

Join rounds with slip stitch unless otherwise stated.

Chain-4 at beginning of row counts as a double crochet and a chain-1 space.

INSTRUCTIONS
WRAP

Row 1: With light blue, ch 270, dc in 5th ch from hook *(beg 4 sk chs counts as a dc and ch-1 sp)*, *ch 1, sk next ch, dc in next ch, rep from * 65 times, ch 1, (dc, ch 1, dc *(mark dc)*, ch 1, dc) in next ch *(dc-center group made)*, ch 1, dc in next ch, *ch 1, sk next ch, dc in next ch, rep from * across, turn. *(67 dc each side of dc-center group)*

Row 2: Ch 1, sc in first dc, tr in next ch-1 sp, *sc in next dc, tr in next ch-1 sp, rep from * to marked dc, (sc, dc *(mark dc)*, sc) in marked dc *(sc-center group made)*, *tr in next ch-1 sp, sc in next dc, rep from * across to beg 4 sk chs, tr in sp formed by beg 4 sk chs, sc in 3rd ch of beg ch-4, **changing colors** *(see Stitch Guide)* to medium blue, turn. *(68 tr each side of marked dc)*

Row 3: Ch 4 *(see Pattern Notes)*, sk next tr, dc in next sc, ch 1, sk next tr, dc in next sc, rep from * to marked dc, work dc-center group in marked dc, dc in next sc, *ch 1, sk next tr, dc in next sc, rep from * across, turn. *(69 dc each side of dc-center group)*

Row 4: Ch 1, sc in first dc, tr in next ch-1 sp, *sc in next dc, tr in next ch-1 sp, rep from * to marked dc, (sc, dc *(mark dc)*, sc) in marked dc *(sc-center group made)*, *tr in next ch-1 sp, sc in next dc, rep from * across to beg ch-4, tr in sp formed by beg ch-4, sc in 3rd ch of same ch-4, change to dark blue, turn. *(70 tr each side of marked dc)*

Rows 5 & 6: Rep rows 3 and 4. At end of row 6, change to navy.

Rows 7 & 8: Rep rows 3 and 4. At end of row 8, change to light blue.

Rows 9 & 10: Rep rows 3 and 4. At end of row 10, change to medium blue.

Rows 11–18: Rep rows 3–10, increasing 1 dc or tr each side of center group. *(84 tr each side of dc-center group)*

Rows 19–24: Rep rows 3–8, increasing 1 dc or tr each side of center group. At end of last row, fasten off. *(90 tr each side of dc-center group)* ∎

Glove Trims

DESIGNS BY **SHIRLEY PATTERSON**

SKILL LEVEL

EASY

FINISHED SIZES

Cuff Trim: ¾ inch x 8 inches
Leaf Trim: ½ inch x 1 inch

MATERIALS

- Aunt Lydia's Classic Crochet size 10 crochet cotton (400 yds):
  4 yds #419 ecru
- Size 9/1.25mm steel crochet hook
- Tapestry needle
- Pair of purchase gloves
- 5mm clear pearl beads: 26

GAUGE

Gauge not important for this project.

PATTERN NOTES

Weave in ends as work progresses.

Join with slip stitch unless otherwise stated.

SPECIAL STITCHES

Cluster (cl): Ch 5, yo twice, insert hook in 5th ch from hook, yo, draw lp up ½-inch, [yo, draw through 2 lps on hook] twice, yo twice, insert hook in same ch, yo, draw lp up ½-inch, [yo, draw through 2 lps on hook] twice, yo, draw through 3 lps on hook (center), ch 5, yo twice, insert hook in 5th ch from hook, yo, draw lp up ½-inch, [yo, draw through 2 lps on hook] twice, yo twice, insert hook in same ch, yo, draw lp up ½-inch, [yo, draw through 2 lps on hook] twice, yo, draw through 3 lps on hook.

Bead cluster (bead cl): Sc in indicated sp, slide bead up close to hook, ch 5, yo twice, insert hook in 5th ch from hook, yo, draw lp up ½-inch, [yo, draw through 2 lps on hook] twice, yo twice, insert hook in same ch, yo, draw lp up ½-inch, [yo, draw through 2 lps on hook] twice, yo, draw through 3 lps on hook (center), ch 5, yo twice, insert hook in 5th ch from hook, yo, draw lp up ½-inch, [yo, draw through 2 lps on hook] twice, yo twice, insert hook in same ch, yo, draw lp up ½-inch, [yo, draw through 2 lps on hook] twice, yo, draw through 3 lps on hook.

INSTRUCTIONS
CUFF TRIM
MAKE 2.

Note: Thread 12 beads on crochet cotton.

Rnd 1 (RS): Hold 1 glove flat with fingers pointing upward, **join** *(see Pattern Notes)* crochet cotton in right-hand fold of edge of glove, ch 1, sc in same sp, **cl** *(see Special Stitches)*, working around edge of glove, *sc in edge ½-inch from previous sc, cl, rep from * 10 times, join in beg sc. *(12 cl)*

Rnd 2: Sl st in each of next 5 chs, **bead cl** *(see Special Stitches)* in same ch as last sl st, bead cl in center of each cl around, join in same sl st as beg bead cl made. Fasten off. *(12 bead cl)*

LEAF TRIM
MAKE 2.

Ch 7, yo 3 times, insert hook in 7th ch from hook, yo, draw lp up ½-inch, [yo, draw through 2 lps on hook] 3 times, *yo 3 times, insert hook in same ch, yo, draw lp up ½-inch, [yo, draw through 2 lps on hook] 3 times, rep from * twice, yo, draw through 5 lps on hook, ch 3, sl st in top of st just made, ch 6, sl st in same ch of beg ch-7, ch 7, **yo 3 times, insert hook in same ch, yo, draw lp up ½-inch, [yo, draw through 2 lps on hook] 3 times, rep from ** 3 times, yo, draw through 4 lps on hook, ch 3, sl st in top of st just made, ch 6, sl st in same ch of beg ch-7. Fasten off.

FINISHING

Sew 1 bead to center of each Leaf Trim. Referring to photo for placement, sew 1 Leaf Trim to each glove. ∎

Easy Anywhere Bag

DESIGN BY **MARTY MILLER**

SKILL LEVEL

EASY

FINISHED SIZE
16 inches x 12 inches, excluding handles

MATERIALS
- Lily Sugar 'n Cream medium (worsted) weight cotton yarn (2½ oz/120 yds/71g per ball): 1 ball each #00083 cornflower blue, #00004 ecru, #00082 jute, #00084 sage green, #01009 soft teal, #00026 light blue, #00042 tea rose and #00003 cream
- Size H/8/5mm crochet hook or size needed to obtain gauge
- Tapestry needle

GAUGE
14 sc = 4 inches; 16 sc rows = 4 inches

PATTERN NOTES
Join with slip stitch unless otherwise stated.

Bag is made in one piece, worked side to side, from one side seam to the other. Front and back are worked at same time, and handles are added on as front and back are worked.

Change colors as desired. Tie a secure knot, and let ends hang out on RS of bag.

Two ways to start the bag are given. Method 1 uses the foundation chain as usual. Method 2 uses the single crochet foundation stitch. Use whichever method you like.

SPECIAL STITCHES
Beginning single crochet foundation st (beg sc foundation st): Ch 2, insert hook in 2nd ch from hook, yo, draw lp through, yo, draw through 1 lp on hook *(base ch completed)*, yo, draw through 2 lps on hook.

Single crochet foundation st (sc foundation st): *Insert hook in last base ch completed or last stitch made, yo, draw lp through, yo, draw through 1 lp on hook *(base ch)*, yo, draw through 2 lps on hook, rep from * until desired number of sts have been completed. *(The ch-2 at beg of row does NOT count as a sc foundation st.).*
To add a sc foundation st to a row, the first sc foundation st is started by inserting hook in same st as last sc worked. Continue as above.

INSTRUCTIONS
METHOD 1
Foundation row: With cornflower blue, ch 43, sc in 2nd ch from hook, sc in each rem ch across, working in unused lps on opposite side of foundation ch, sc in each lp, turn. *(84 sc)*

Beg with row 1 following Method 2 foundation row.

METHOD 2
Foundation row: With desired color, work **beg sc foundation st** *(see Special Stitches)*, work **sc foundation st** *(see Special Stitches)* 41 times, working on opposite side of row, sc in each st, turn. *(84 sc)*

BOTH METHODS
Row 1 (RS): Ch 1, sc in each sc across, turn.

Rows 2–11: Rep row 1.

METHOD 1
Row 12: Ch 1, sc in each sc across, ch 43, turn. *(84 sc, 43 chs)*

Row 13: Ch 1, sc in 2nd ch from hook, sc in each rem ch, sc in each sc across, ch 43, turn. *(126 sc, 43 chs)*

Row 14: Ch 1, sc in 2nd ch from hook, sc in each rem ch, sc in each sc across, turn. *(168 sc)*

METHOD 2
Row 12: Ch 1, sc in each sc across, work 42 sc foundation sts, turn. *(84 sc, 42 sc foundation st)*

Row 13: Ch 1, sc in each sc foundation st and in each sc across, work 42 sc foundation sts, turn. *(126 sc, 42 sc foundation st)*

Row 14: Ch 1, sc in each sc foundation st and in each sc across, turn. *(168 sc)*

BOTH METHODS
Row 15: Ch 1, sc in each sc across, turn.

Rows 16–19: Rep row 15.

Row 20: Ch 1, sc in each of first 126 sc, turn, leaving rem sc unworked. *(126 sc)*

Row 21: Ch 1, sc in each of first 84 sc, turn, leaving rem sc unworked. *(84 sc)*

Rows 22–47: Rep row 1.

METHOD 1
Row 48: Ch 1, sc in each sc across, ch 43, turn. *(84 sc, 43 chs)*

Row 49: Ch 1, sc in 2nd ch from hook, sc in each rem ch, sc in each sc across, ch 43, turn. *(126 sc, 43 chs)*

Row 50: Ch 1, sc in 2nd ch from hook, sc in each rem ch, sc in each sc across, turn. *(168 sc)*

METHOD 2

Row 48: Ch 1, sc in each sc across, work 42 sc foundation sts, turn. *(84 sc, 42 sc foundation st)*

Row 49: Ch 1, sc in each sc foundation st and in each sc across, work 42 sc foundation sts, turn. *(126 sc, 42 sc foundation st)*

Row 50: Ch 1, sc in each sc foundation st and in each sc across, turn. *(168 sc)*

BOTH METHODS

Row 51: Ch 1, sc in each sc across, turn.

Rows 52–55: Rep row 51.

Row 56: Ch 1, sc in each of first 126 sc, turn, leaving rem sc unworked. *(126 sc)*

Row 57: Ch 1, sc in each of first 84 sc, turn, leaving rem sc unworked. *(84 sc)*

Rows 58–67: Rep row 1. Do not fasten off.

ASSEMBLY

Turn Bag inside out. Hold last row and foundation row tog, carefully matching sts. Working through both lps of sts on rows at same time, sc in each sc across. Fasten off. Turn Bag right-side out.

For each handle, hold 2 ends of rows of long pieces from 1 side of bag with WS tog. Join matching color with sl st in end of first row, ch 1, working across ends of rows and through both pieces at same time, sc in each row across. Fasten off. ■

Flame Necklace

DESIGN BY **JENNY KING**

SKILL LEVEL

INTERMEDIATE

FINISHED SIZE
22 inches long

MATERIALS
- Ribbon/novelty yarn small enough to thread size 6 beads:
    25g orange
- Size E/4/3.5mm crochet hook
- Size 10/1.1.5mm steel crochet hook
- Tapestry needle
- Beading needle
- ¾-inch plastic rings: 2
- Size 6 seed beads: 204
- 1 magnetic clasp

GAUGE
Gauge not important to this project.

PATTERN NOTES
Weave in ends as work progresses.

Join with slip stitch unless otherwise stated.

INSTRUCTIONS
Note: Thread all beads on yarn before beginning project.

With size E hook, **join** *(see Pattern Notes)* yarn in first plastic ring, 10 sc in ring, ch 10, change to size 10 steel hook, sc in hole in end of 1 magnetic clasp, change to size E hook, ch 10, 10 sc in ring.

Strand 1: Ch 2, slide bead close to hook, [ch 3, slide bead close to hook] 49 times, ch 2, 2 sc in 2nd plastic ring, turn.

Strand 2: Ch 9, slide bead close to hook, [ch 10, slide bead close to hook] 14 times, ch 9, 2 sc in first ring next to last 2 sc, turn.

Strand 3: Ch 19, slide bead close to hook, [ch 20, slide bead close to hook] 6 times, ch 19, 2 sc in 2nd ring next to last 2 sc, turn.

Strand 4: Ch 14, slide bead close to hook, [ch 15, slide bead close to hook] 9 times, ch 15, 2 sc in first ring next to last 2 sc, turn.

Strand 5: Ch 9, slide bead close to hook, [ch 10, slide bead close to hook] 14 times, ch 9, 2 sc in 2nd ring next to last 2 sc, turn.

Strand 6: Ch 4, slide bead close to hook, [ch 5, slide bead close to hook] 29 times, ch 4, 2 sc in first ring next to last 2 sc, turn.

Strand 7: Ch 19, slide bead close to hook, [ch 20, slide bead close to hook] 6 times, ch 20, 2 sc in 2nd ring next to last 2 sc, turn.

Strand 8: Ch 14, slide bead close to hook, [ch 15, slide bead close to hook] 9 times, ch 14, 2 sc in first ring next to last 2 sc, turn.

Strand 9: Ch 19, slide bead close to hook, [ch 20, slide bead close to hook] 6 times, ch 20, 2 sc in 2nd ring next to last 2 sc, turn.

Strand 10: Ch 5, slide bead close to hook, [ch 7, slide bead close to hook] 20 times, ch 7, 2 sc in first ring next to last 2 sc, turn.

Strand 11: Ch 14, slide bead close to hook, [ch 15, slide bead close to hook] 9 times, ch 15, 2 sc in 2nd ring next to last 2 sc, turn.

Strand 12: Ch 19, slide bead close to hook, [ch 20, slide bead close to hook] 6 times, ch 20, 2 sc in first ring next to last 2 sc, turn.

Strand 13: Ch 9, slide bead close to hook, [ch 10, slide bead close to hook] 14 times, ch 10, 10 sc in 2nd ring next to last 2 sc, change to size 10 steel hook, sc in hole on opposite side of magnetic clasp, change to size E hook, ch 10, 10 sc in 2nd ring, join in beg sc. Fasten off. ■

Turtle

DESIGN BY KATHLEEN STUART

SKILL LEVEL

■■□□
EASY

FINISHED SIZE
5 inches x 7 inches

MATERIALS
- Red Heart Kids medium (worsted) weight yarn (solids: 5 oz/290 yds/141g per skein; multis: 4 oz/ 232 yds/113g per skein):
  1 skein each #2940 beach multi and #2652 lime
- Medium (worsted) weight yarn: 3 oz/150 yds/85g green
- Size G/6/4mm crochet hook or size needed to obtain gauge
- Black 6mm eyes: 2
- Tapestry needle
- Stitch marker
- Polyester fiberfill

GAUGE
Rnds 1 & 2 = 1 inch

PATTERN NOTES
Weave in ends as work progresses.

Join with slip stitch as indicated unless otherwise stated.

Chain-3 at beginning of round counts as first double crochet.

INSTRUCTIONS
TURTLE
HEAD & BODY
Note: Head and Body are worked in continuous rnds. Do not join unless specified; mark beg of rnds.

Rnd 1 (RS): Starting at face with green, ch 2, 6 sc in 2nd ch from hook. *(6 sc)*

Rnd 2: 2 sc in each sc around. *(12 sc)*

Rnd 3: [Sc in next sc, 2 sc in next st] 6 times. *(18 sc)*

Rnd 4: [Sc in each of next 2 sc, 2 sc in next sc] 6 times. *(24 sc)*

Rnd 5: Sc in each sc around.

Rnd 6: Rep rnd 5.

Rnd 7: [Sc in each of next 2 sc, **sc dec** *(see Stitch Guide)* in next 2 sc] 6 times. *(18 sc)*

Note: Place eyes between rnds 3 and 4 about 2 sc apart.

Rnds 8 & 9: Rep rnd 5.

Rnd 10: [Sc in next sc, sc dec in next 2 sc] 6 times. *(12 sc)*

Rnds 11–13: Rep rnd 5.

Stuff with fiberfill.

Rnd 14: [Sc in next sc, 2 sc in next sc] 6 times. *(18 sc)*

Rnd 15: Rep rnd 5.

Rnd 16: 2 sc in each sc around. *(36 sc)*

Rnd 17: Sc in each of next 6 sc, sk next 6 sc *(front leg opening)*, sc in each of next 12 sc, sk next 6 sc *(front leg opening)*, sc in each of last 6 sc. *(24 sc)*

Rnds 18–22: Rep rnd 5.

Rnd 23: Sc in each of next 5 sc, ch 3, sk next 3 sc *(back leg opening)*, sc in each of next 9 sc, ch 3, sk next 3 sc *(back leg opening)*, sc in each of last 4 sc.

Rnd 24: Sc in each sc around, sk ch sts. *(18 sc)*

Stuff with fiberfill.

Rnd 25: [Sc in next sc, sc dec in next 2 sc] 6 times. *(12 sc)*

Rnd 26: [Sc in each of next 2 sc, sc dec in next 2 sc] 3 times. *(9 sc)*

Rnd 27: Rep rnd 5.

TAIL
Rnd 28: [Sc in next sc, sc dec in next 2 sc] 3 times. *(6 sc)*

Rnds 29 & 30: Rep rnd 5.

Stuff with fiberfill.

Rnd 31: [Sc dec in next 2 sc] 3 times. Leaving an 8-inch end for sewing, fasten off. *(3 sc)*

FRONT LEG
MAKE 2.
Note: Piece is worked in continuous rnds. Do not join unless specified; mark beg of rnds.

Rnd 1 (RS): Join green with sc in first sc of first 6 sk sc on rnd 16 of Body, sc in same sc, 2 sc in each of next 5 sk sc. *(12 sc)*

Rnd 2: Sc in each sc around.

Rnds 3–6: Rep rnd 2.

Stuff with small amount of fiberfill.

Rnd 7: [Sc dec in next 2 sc] 6 times. Leaving an 8-inch end for sewing, fasten off. *(6 sc)*

Work 2nd Leg in same manner in 2nd group of 6 sk sc on rnd 16.

BACK LEG
MAKE 2.
Note: Piece is worked in continuous rnds. Do not join unless specified; mark beg of rnds.

Rnd 1 (RS): Join green with sc in first sc of first 3 sk sc on rnd 23 of Body, sc in same sc, 2 sc in each of next 2 sk sc, 2 sc in each of next 3 chs. *(12 sc)*

Rnd 2: Sc in each sc around.

Rnds 3–6: Rep rnd 2.

Stuff with small amount of fiberfill.

Rnd 7: [Sc dec in next 2 sc] 6 times. Fasten off. *(6 sc)*

Work 2nd Leg in same manner in 2nd group of 3 sk sc and ch-3 sp on rnd 23.

SHELL
MAKE 1 BEACH AND 1 LIME GREEN.
MOTIF
MAKE 6.
Ch 4, **join** *(see Pattern Notes)* in first ch to form a ring, **ch 3** *(see Pattern Notes)*, 2 dc in ring, ch 2, [3 dc in ring, ch 2] 4 times, join in 3rd ch of beg ch-3. Fasten off.

ASSEMBLY
Arrange beach Motifs according to diagram. To join Motifs, hold 2 Motifs with RS tog. Working through both thicknesses at same time and in **back lps** *(see Stitch Guide)*, join matching yarn with sc in 2nd ch of 1 ch-2 sp, sc in each of next 3 dc, sc in next ch of next ch-2 sp. Fasten off. Rep with rem Motifs.

LEG OPENING
MAKE 4.
Referring to diagram, join matching yarn in marked ch-2 sp of 1 Motif, ch 10, sl st in next marked ch-2 sp on same Motif. Fasten off. Rep on 3 rem marked Motifs.

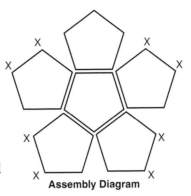

Assembly Diagram

FINISHING
With end left for sewing, sew end of Tail closed.

Using **backstitches** (*Fig. 1*), with black, embroider smile.

Using **French knots** (*Fig. 2*), with black, embroider 2 eyes on face.

Place Shell on Turtle, having Motif without Leg Opening over tail. ■

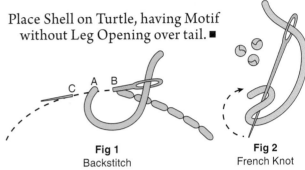

Fig 1
Backstitch

Fig 2
French Knot

Bunny Booties

DESIGN BY **JENNY KING**

SKILL LEVEL

EASY

FINISHED SIZES
Instructions given fit 0–3 months; changes for 6–12 months and 18 months–2 years are in [ ].

MATERIALS
- Fingering (sock) weight washable wool yarn:
  10 yds off-white
  2 yds pink
- Size D/3.25/3mm crochet hook or size needed to obtain gauge
- Tapestry needle

GAUGE
8 sts = 1 inch

PATTERN NOTE
Weave in ends as work progresses.

INSTRUCTIONS
BOOTIE
MAKE 2.
SQUARE
MAKE 4.
Row 1 (RS): With off-white, ch 26 [30, 36], sc in 4th ch from hook, ch 1, sk next ch, *sc in next ch, ch 1, sk next ch, rep from * across to last ch, sc in last ch, turn. (*12 [14, 17] sc, 11 [13, 16] ch-1 sps*)

Row 2: Ch 2, sk first sc, *sc in next ch-1 sp, ch 1, sk next sc, rep from * across to beg 3 sk chs, sc in sp formed by beg 3 sk chs, turn.

Row 3: Ch 2, sk first sc, *sc in next ch-1 sp, ch 1, sk next sc, rep from * across to beg ch-2 sp, sc in beg ch-2 sp, turn.

Rows 4–24 [4–27, 4–33]: Rep row 3. At end of last row, fasten off.

EAR
MAKE 4.
Row 1 (RS): Leaving an 8-inch end, ch 8, sc in 4th ch from hook, ch 1, sk next ch, sc in next ch, ch 1, sk next ch, sc in last ch, turn. *(3 sc, 2 ch-1 sps)*

Row 2: Ch 2, sk first sc, [sc in next ch-1 sp, ch 1] twice, sc in sp formed by beg 3 sk chs, turn.

Row 3: Ch 2, sk first sc, [sc in next ch-1 sp, ch 1] twice, sc in beg ch-2 sp, turn.

Rows 4–8: Rep row 3. At end of last row, fasten off.

FINISHING
Step 1: Referring to diagrams, fold and sew Squares.

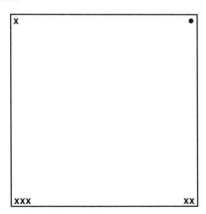

Diagram 1

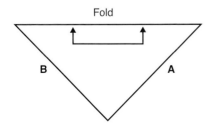

Diagram 2

Step 2: On each Ear, weave long end through row 1, gather and secure end. Sew in place on Booties.

Step 3: Using **bouillion stitch** *(see Fig. 1)*, with pink, embroider eyes and nose. ∎

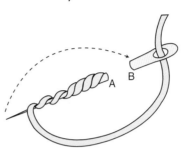

Fig. 1
Bullion Stitch
Bring needle up at A, wrap yarn around needle 10 times, take needle down at B, then back up at A.

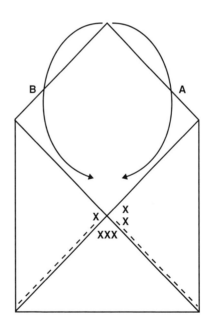

Diagram 3

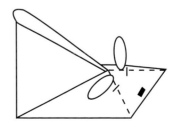

Diagram 4
Side View

Scrap Jacket

DESIGN BY **DARLA SIMS**

SKILL LEVEL

EASY

FINISHED SIZES
Instructions given fit size small; changes for medium and large are in [ ].

FINISHED GARMENT MEASUREMENTS
Chest: 27 inches *(small)*, 29 inches *(medium)*, 31 inches *(large)*

MATERIALS
- Medium (worsted) weight yarn: 20 [22, 24] oz/1000 [1100, 1200] yds/283g various colors
- Size H/8/5mm crochet hook or size needed to obtain gauge
- Tapestry needle

GAUGE
7 sts = 2 inches

PATTERN NOTES
Weave in ends as work progresses.

Join with slip stitch unless otherwise stated.

Chain-2 at beginning of row or round counts as first half double crochet.

INSTRUCTIONS
JACKET
LOWER BODY
Note: Lower Body is worked from side to side. Change color at end of every 2nd row.

Row 1 (RS): With color of choice, ch 31 [37, 41], hdc in 3rd ch from hook *(beg 2 sk chs count as a hdc)*, hdc in each of next 14 [17, 19] chs, dc in each of next 15 [18, 20] chs, turn. *(30 [36, 40] sts)*

Row 2: Ch 8, 3 sc in 2nd ch from hook, 3 sc in each of rem ch *(curlicue made)*, dc in each of next 15 [18, 20] sts, hdc in each of next 15 [18, 20] sts, **change color** *(see Stitch Guide)*, turn.

Row 3: Ch 2 *(see Pattern Notes)*, hdc in each of next 14 [17, 29] sts, dc in each of next 15 [18, 20] sts, turn.

Row 4: Ch 8, 3 sc in 2nd ch from hook, 3 sc in each of rem ch *(curlicue made)*, dc in each of next 15 [18, 20] sts, hdc in each of next 15 [18, 20] sts, change color, turn.

Rows 5–80 [5–88, 5–92]: Rep rows 3 and 4 alternately. At end of last row, do not change color. Fasten off.

Row 81 [89, 93]: Hold piece with RS facing and curlicues to bottom, working across end of rows at top of piece, join color of choice in first st, ch 2, work 79 [87, 95] hdc evenly sp across side, turn. *(80 [88, 96] hdc)*

Row 82 [90, 94]: Ch 2, hdc in each hdc across. Change to new color.

RIGHT FRONT YOKE
Row 1 (RS): Ch 1, **hdc dec** *(see Stitch Guide)* in first 2 sts, hdc in each of next 18 [20, 21] sts, turn. *(19 [21, 22] hdc)*

Row 2: Ch 2, hdc in each hdc across, turn.

Rows 3–14: [Rep rows 1 and 2 alternately] 6 times. *(13 [15, 16] hdc at end of last row)*

Row 15: Ch 2, hdc in each hdc across, turn.

Rep row 15 until yoke measures 5½ [6, 6½] inches. Fasten off.

LEFT FRONT YOKE

Row 1 (RS): Hold piece with RS facing, sk next 40 [44, 46] sts on last row of Lower Body from Right Front Yoke, **join** (see Pattern Notes) color of choice in next st, ch 2, hdc in each of next 17 [19, 20] sts, hdc dec in last 2 sts, turn. (19 [21, 22] hdc)

Row 2: Ch 2, hdc in each hdc across, turn.

Rows 3–14: [Rep rows 1 and 2 alternately] 6 times. (13 [15, 16] hdc at end of last row)

Row 15: Ch 2, hdc in each hdc across, turn.

Rep row 15 until yoke measures 5½ [6, 6½] inches. Fasten off.

BACK

Row 1: Hold piece with RS facing, join color of choice in first sk st on last row of Lower Body from Right Front Yoke, ch 2, hdc in each of next 39 [43, 45] sts, turn. (40 [44, 46] hdc)

Row 2: Ch 2, hdc in each hdc across, turn.

Rep row 2 until piece measures same as fronts. Fasten off.

SLEEVE
MAKE 2.

Note: Use different color for each sleeve.

Row 1 (RS): Ch 23 [27, 29], hdc in 3rd ch from hook (beg 2 sk chs count as a hdc), hdc in each rem ch across, turn. (22 [26, 28] hdc)

Row 2: Ch 2, hdc in each hdc across, turn.

Row 3: Ch 2, hdc in first hdc, hdc in each rem hdc to last hdc, 2 hdc in last hdc, turn. (24 [26, 30] hdc)

Rows 4–19 [4–19, 4–21]: [Rep rows 2 and 3 alternately] 7 [7, 8] times. (38 [42, 46] hdc at end of last row)

Row 20 [20, 22]: Ch 2, hdc in each hdc across, turn.

Rep row 20 [20, 22] until piece measures 8½ [10½, 11½] inches. Fasten off.

ASSEMBLY

Sew shoulder seams. Sew sleeve seams. Sew in sleeves, matching center of sleeve to shoulder seam.

SLEEVE EDGING

Note: Use same color for edging as used for last 2 rows of Lower Body.

Hold 1 Sleeve with RS facing, join yarn with sc in seam, sc in each st around, join in beg sc. Fasten off. Rep on rem Sleeve.

FRONT EDGING & TIES

Note: Use same color for edging as used for last 2 rows of Lower Body.

Hold piece with RS facing, join yarn in end of row 81 [89, 93] of Lower Body, ch 38, 3 sc in 2nd ch from hook, 3 sc in each of next 6 chs, sl st in each rem ch, working up yoke section, work 16 [17, 18] sc evenly spaced to shoulder seam, work 14 sc evenly spaced across back, working down yoke section, work 16 [17, 18] sc evenly spaced to row 81 [89, 93] of Lower Body, ch 38, 3 sc in 2nd ch from hook, 3 sc in each of next 6 chs, sl st in each rem ch. Fasten off.

HAT

Note: Work 2 rows each color, following same color sequence as used for Lower Body.

Rnd 1 (RS): Ch 60, **join** (see Pattern Notes) to form a ring, being careful not to twist ch, **ch 2** (see Pattern Notes), hdc in each rem ch around, join in 2nd ch of beg ch-2. (60 hdc)

Rnd 2: Ch 2, hdc in each st around, join in 2nd ch of beg ch-2.

Rnds 3–12: Rep rnd 2. At end of last row, fasten off.

CROWN

Rnd 1: Maintaining color sequence, join yarn in joining of rnd 12, ch 2, ***hdc dec** (see Stitch Guide) in next 2 sts, hdc in next st, rep from * across to last 2 sts, hdc dec in last 2 sts, join in 2nd ch of beg ch-2. (40 hdc)

Rnd 2: Ch 1, hdc in next st, [hdc dec in next 2 sts] 19 times, join in first hdc. **Do not change color.** *(20 hdc)*

Rnd 3: Ch 2, hdc in each st around, join in 2nd ch of beg ch-2.

Rnd 4: Ch 1, hdc dec in first 3 hdc, [hdc dec in next 3 sts] 5 times, hdc dec in next 2 hdc, join in beg st. Fasten off. *(7 hdc)*

CURLICUE
MAKE 7.
Following color sequence and leaving 6-inch end, join yarn in first hdc of rnd 4 of Hat, ch 12, 3 sc in 2nd ch from hook, 3 sc in each of next 7 chs, sl st in each of next 3 chs, sc in same st as joining. Rep in each rem hdc of rnd 4. Pull all ends to inside of Hat. Divide ends in 2 groups and tie in knot on inside of Hat.

HAT EDGING
Hold Hat with RS facing and foundation ch at top, working in unused lps of foundation ch, join same color as Jacket edgings with sc in any st, sc in each rem st around, join in joining sc. Fasten off. ∎

Flower Bib & Booties

DESIGNS BY **YVONNE HEALY**

SKILL LEVEL

EASY

FINISHED SIZES
Bootie sole: 3 inches
Flower bib: 7 inches in diameter

MATERIALS
- Pisgah Yarn & Dyeing Co. Inc. Peaches & Crème medium (worsted) weight cotton yarn (2½ oz/122 yds/71g per skein): 1 skein each #12 gold and #26 light blue
- Sizes F/5/3.75mm and G/6/4mm crochet hooks or sizes needed to obtain gauge
- Tapestry needle

4 MEDIUM

GAUGE
With size F hook: 4 sc = 1 inch
With size G hook: 2 dc rnds = 1¼ inches

PATTERN NOTES
Weave in ends as work progresses.

Join rounds with slip stitch unless otherwise stated.

Chain-3 at beginning of row or round counts as first double crochet.

INSTRUCTIONS
FLOWER BOOTIE
MAKE 2.
Row 1: With size F hook and yellow, ch 4, sc in 2nd ch from hook, sc in each rem ch, turn. *(3 sc)*

Row 2: Ch 1, sc in each sc across, turn.

Rows 3 & 4: Rep row 2.

Row 5: Ch 1, 2 sc in first sc, sc in next sc, 2 sc in last sc, turn. *(5 sc)*

Rows 6–10: Rep row 2.

Row 11: Ch 1, sc in each sc across,

Rnd 12: Now working in rnds, ch 1, work 11 sc across ends of rows, working in unused lps on opposite side of foundation ch, sc in each of next 3 lps, work 11 sc across ends of rows on next side, sc in each of next 5 sc on row 11, **join** *(see Pattern Notes)* in **back lp** *(see Stitch Guide)* of beg sc. *(30 sc)*

Rnd 13: Ch 1, sc in same lp as joining, working in back lps, sc in each rem sc around, join in beg sc.

Rnd 14: Ch 1, sc in same sc as joining, ch 1, sc in each of next 9 sc, [**sc dec** *(see Stitch Guide)* in next 2 sc] 5 times, sc in each of next 10 sc, join in beg sc. *(25 sc)*

Rnd 15: Ch 1, sc in same sc as joining, ch 1, sc in each of next 7 sc, [sc dec in next 2 sc] 5 times, sc in each of next 7 sc, join in back lp of beg sc. *(20 sc)*

Rnd 16: Rep rnd 13.

Rnd 17: Ch 1, sc in same sc as joining, ch 1, sc in each of next 6 sc, [sc dec in next 2 sc] 3 times, sc in each of next 7 sc, join in of beg sc. *(17 sc)*

Rnd 18: Ch 1, sc in each sc around, join in beg sc.

Rnds 19–22: Rep rnd 18. At end of last rnd, fasten off.

FLOWER
MAKE 2.

Rnd 1: With size F hook and yellow, ch 4, join in first ch to form ring, ch 1, 7 sc in ring, join in beg sc. Fasten off. *(7 sc)*

Rnd 2: Join light blue in any sc, ch 1, (sc, tr, sc) in same sc, (sc, tr, sc) in each rem sc around, join in beg sc. Fasten off.

FINISHING
Sew Flower to center front of each Bootie.

FLOWER BIB

Rnd 1: With size G hook and yellow, ch 4, 13 dc in 4th ch from hook *(beg 3 sk chs count as a dc)*, join in 3rd ch of beg ch-3. *(14 dc)*

Rnd 2: **Ch 3** *(see Pattern Notes)*, dc in same ch as joining, 2 dc in each rem dc around, join in 3rd ch of beg ch-3. *(28 dc)*

Rnd 3: Ch 3, dc in same ch as joining, [dc in each of next 2 dc, 2 dc in next dc] 9 times, join in 3rd ch of beg ch-3. *(38 dc)*

Rnd 4: Ch 3, dc in same ch as joining, [dc in each of next 3 dc, 2 dc in next dc] 9 times, dc in last dc, join in 3rd ch of beg ch-3. Fasten off. *(48 dc)*

Rnd 5: Join light blue in any dc, ch 1, sc in each dc around, join in beg sc.

Rnd 6: Ch 1, sc in same sc, sc in next sc, (2 dc, tr, 2 dc) in next sc, *sc in each of next 2 sc, (2 dc, tr, 2 dc) in next sc, rep from * around, join in beg sc.

Rnd 7: Ch 1, sc in each of first 4 sts, [3 sc in next tr, sc in each of next 6 sts] 15 times, 3 sc in next tr, sc in each of next 2 sc, join in beg sc. Fasten off. ■

Teddy Bear

DESIGN BY **DARLA SIMS**

Party Pinafore

SKILL LEVEL

EASY

FINISHED SIZE
Fits 15-inch teddy bear

MATERIALS
- Medium (worsted) weight yarn:
  1 oz/50 yds/28g each white, pink and purple
- Size H/8/5mm crochet hook or size needed to obtain gauge
- Tapestry needle
- Stitch markers

GAUGE
7 sts = 2 inches

PATTERN NOTES
Weave in ends as work progresses.

Join with slip stitch unless otherwise stated.

Chain-3 at beginning of row or round counts as first double crochet.

INSTRUCTIONS
PINAFORE
SKIRT
Row 1 (RS): With pink, ch 49, 2 dc in 5th ch from hook (*beg 4 sk chs count as a dc*), *sk next ch, 2 dc in next ch, rep from * across to last 2 chs, sk next ch, dc in last ch. Fasten off. *(46 dc)*

Row 2: With RS facing, join purple with sc between first 2 dc, *ch 1, sk next 2 dc, sc between last and next dc, rep from * across, working last sc between last 2 dc. Fasten off. *(23 sc, 22 ch-1 sps)*

Row 3: **Join** (*see Pattern Notes*) pink in 4th ch of beg 4 sk chs on row 1, **ch 3** (*see Pattern Notes*), 2 dc in each ch-1 sp across, 2 dc in last dc. Fasten off. *(46 dc)*

Row 4: With white, rep row 2.

Row 5: Join pink in 3rd ch of beg ch-3 of row 3, ch 3, 2 dc in each ch-1 sp across, 2 dc in last dc. Fasten off. *(46 dc)*

Row 6: With purple, rep row 2.

Row 7: Join pink in 3rd ch of beg ch-3 of row 5, ch 3, 2 dc in each ch-1 sp across, 2 dc in last dc, turn. *(46 dc)*

Row 8: Ch 1, sk first dc, [**sc dec** (*see Stitch Guide*) in next 2 dc] 22 times, sc in 3rd ch of beg ch-3. **Do not fasten off.** Remove hook. *(23 sc)*

TIES & WAISTBAND
With RS facing, join separate length of pink in first st of row 8, ch 30 (*tie made*). Fasten off. Insert hook in dropped lp, ch 31 (*tie made*), sc in 2nd ch from hook, sc in each rem ch, sc in each sc, sc in each ch of next ch-30. Fasten off. *(83 sc)*

Note: Mark 31st and 53rd sc.

BIB
Row 1 (WS): With WS facing, sk first 37 sc, join pink with sc in next st, sc in each of next 8 sc, turn. *(9 sc)*

Row 2: Ch 1, sc in each sc across, turn.

Rows 3 & 4: Rep row 2. At end of last row, fasten off.

SKIRT RUFFLE
Hold Skirt with RS facing and foundation ch at top, working in unused lps of foundation ch, join white in first lp, ch 3, 2 dc in same lp, 3 dc in each rem lp across. Fasten off.

STRAPS & RUFFLES
FIRST STRAP
Hold Bib with RS facing, join pink in first st on last row of Bib, ch 15, sl st in 31st marked st on Waistband, ch 1, turn, sc in each ch, sl st in same st as beg sl st made. Fasten off.

RUFFLE
Join white in end of row 1 of Bib, ch 3, 2 dc in same sp, 3 dc in end of each of next 3 rows, working in unused lps of foundation ch of First Strap, 3 dc in each ch. Fasten off.

2ND STRAP
Hold Skirt with RS facing, join pink in 53rd marked st on Waistband, ch 15, sl st in last st on last row of Bib, ch 1, turn, sc in each ch, sl st in same st as beg sl st made. Fasten off.

RUFFLE
Working in unused lps of foundation ch of 2nd Strap, join white in first lp, ch 3, 2 dc in same lp, 3 dc in each rem lp, 3 sc in end of each of next 4 rows of Bib. Fasten off.

FLOWER
With purple, ch 7, sl st in 7th ch from hook, [ch 6, sl st in same ch] 11 times. Fasten off.

FINISHING
Sew Flower to Bib.

HAT
Rnd 1: With purple, ch 4, 7 dc in 4th ch from hook *(beg 3 sk chs count as a dc)*, join in 3rd ch of beg 3 sk chs. *(8 dc)*

Rnd 2: Ch 3, dc in same st as joining, 2 dc in each of next 7 dc, join in 3rd ch of beg ch-3. *(16 dc)*

Rnd 3: Ch 3, 2 dc in next st, [dc in next st, 2 dc in next st] 7 times, join in 3rd ch of beg ch-3. *(24 dc)*

Rnd 4: Ch 3, dc in next st, 2 dc in next st, [dc in each of next 2 sts, 2 dc in next st] 7 times, join in 3rd ch of beg ch-3. *(32 dc)*

Rnd 5: Ch 3, dc in next 2 sts, 2 dc in next st, [dc in each of next 3 sts, 2 dc in next st] 7 times, join in 3rd ch of beg ch-3. Fasten off. *(40 dc)*

Rnd 6: Join white in same ch as joining, ch 3, 2 dc in same ch, 3 dc in each dc around, join in 3rd ch of beg ch-3. Fasten off.

TIE
With pink, make a 22-inch chain. Fasten off.

FINISHING
Weave Tie through rnd 5 of Hat and tie in bow. ∎

Stitch Guide
For more complete information, visit **FreePatterns.com**

ABBREVIATIONS

beg	begin/begins/beginning
bpdc	back post double crochet
bpsc	back post single crochet
bptr	back post treble crochet
CC	contrasting color
ch(s)	chain(s)
ch-	refers to chain or space previously made (e.g., ch-1 space)
ch sp(s)	chain space(s)
cl(s)	cluster(s)
cm	centimeter(s)
dc	double crochet (singular/plural)
dc dec	double crochet 2 or more stitches together, as indicated
dec	decrease/decreases/decreasing
dtr	double treble crochet
ext	extended
fpdc	front post double crochet
fpsc	front post single crochet
fptr	front post treble crochet
g	gram(s)
hdc	half double crochet
hdc dec	half double crochet 2 or more stitches together, as indicated
inc	increase/increases/increasing
lp(s)	loop(s)
MC	main color
mm	millimeter(s)
oz	ounce(s)
pc	popcorn(s)
rem	remain/remains/remaining
rep(s)	repeat(s)
rnd(s)	round(s)
RS	right side
sc	single crochet (singular/plural)
sc dec	single crochet 2 or more stitches together, as indicated
sk	skip/skipped/skipping
sl st(s)	slip stitch(es)
sp(s)	space/spaces/spaced
st(s)	stitch(es)
tog	together
tr	treble crochet
trtr	triple treble crochet
WS	wrong side
yd(s)	yard(s)
yo	yarn over

Chain—ch: Yo, pull through lp on hook.

Slip stitch—sl st: Insert hook in st, pull through both lps on hook.

Single crochet—sc: Insert hook in st, yo, pull through st, yo, pull through both lps on hook.

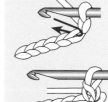

Front post stitch—fp: **Back post stitch—bp:** When working post st, insert hook from right to left around post st on previous row.

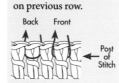

Front loop—front lp **Back loop—back lp**

Front Loop   Back Loop

Half double crochet— hdc: Yo, insert hook in st, yo, pull through st, yo, pull through all 3 lps on hook.

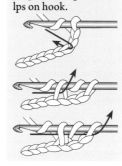

Double crochet—dc: Yo, insert hook in st, yo, pull through st, [yo, pull through 2 lps] twice.

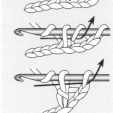

Change colors: Drop first color; with 2nd color, pull through last 2 lps of st.

Treble crochet—tr: Yo twice, insert hook in st, yo, pull through st, [yo, pull through 2 lps] 3 times.

Double treble crochet—dtr: Yo 3 times, insert hook in st, yo, pull through st, [yo, pull through 2 lps] 4 times.

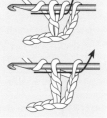

Single crochet decrease (sc dec): (Insert hook, yo, draw lp through) in each of the sts indicated, yo, draw through all lps on hook.

Example of 2-sc dec

Half double crochet decrease (hdc dec): (Yo, insert hook, yo, draw lp through) in each of the sts indicated, yo, draw through all lps on hook.

Example of 2-hdc dec

Double crochet decrease (dc dec): (Yo, insert hook, yo, draw loop through, draw through 2 lps on hook) in each of the sts indicated, yo, draw through all lps on hook.

Example of 2-dc dec

Treble crochet decrease (tr dec): Holding back last lp of each st, tr in each of the sts indicated, yo, pull through all lps on hook.

Example of 2-tr dec

US		UK
sl st (slip stitch)	=	sc (single crochet)
sc (single crochet)	=	dc (double crochet)
hdc (half double crochet)	=	htr (half treble crochet)
dc (double crochet)	=	tr (treble crochet)
tr (treble crochet)	=	dtr (double treble crochet)
dtr (double treble crochet)	=	ttr (triple treble crochet)
skip	=	miss

Metric Conversion Charts

METRIC CONVERSIONS

yards	x	.9144	=	metres (m)
yards	x	91.44	=	centimetres (cm)
inches	x	2.54	=	centimetres (cm)
inches	x	25.40	=	millimetres (mm)
inches	x	.0254	=	metres (m)

centimetres	x	.3937	=	inches
metres	x	1.0936	=	yards

INCHES INTO MILLIMETRES & CENTIMETRES (Rounded off slightly)

inches	mm	cm	inches	cm	inches	cm	inches	cm
1/8	3	0.3	5	12.5	21	53.5	38	96.5
1/4	6	0.6	5 1/2	14	22	56	39	99
3/8	10	1	6	15	23	58.5	40	101.5
1/2	13	1.3	7	18	24	61	41	104
5/8	15	1.5	8	20.5	25	63.5	42	106.5
3/4	20	2	9	23	26	66	43	109
7/8	22	2.2	10	25.5	27	68.5	44	112
1	25	2.5	11	28	28	71	45	114.5
1 1/4	32	3.2	12	30.5	29	73.5	46	117
1 1/2	38	3.8	13	33	30	76	47	119.5
1 3/4	45	4.5	14	35.5	31	79	48	122
2	50	5	15	38	32	81.5	49	124.5
2 1/2	65	6.5	16	40.5	33	84	50	127
3	75	7.5	17	43	34	86.5		
3 1/2	90	9	18	46	35	89		
4	100	10	19	48.5	36	91.5		
4 1/2	115	11.5	20	51	37	94		

KNITTING NEEDLES CONVERSION CHART

Canada/U.S.	0	1	2	3	4	5	6	7	8	9	10	10½	11	13	15
Metric (mm)	2	2¼	2¾	3¼	3½	3¾	4	4½	5	5½	6	6½	8	9	10

CROCHET HOOKS CONVERSION CHART

Canada/U.S.	1/B	2/C	3/D	4/E	5/F	6/G	8/H	9/I	10/J	10½/K	N
Metric (mm)	2.25	2.75	3.25	3.5	3.75	4.25	5	5.5	6	6.5	9.0

TOLL-FREE ORDER LINE or to request a free catalog (800) LV-ANNIE (800) 582-6643
Customer Service (800) AT-ANNIE (800) 282-6643, **Fax** (800) 882-6643
Visit AnniesAttic.com
We have made every effort to ensure the accuracy and completeness of these instructions.
We cannot, however, be responsible for human error, typographical mistakes or variations in individual work.

ISBN: 978-1-59635-289-6

Printed in USA

2 3 4 5 6 7 8 9